Safety across the curriculum

I wish to dedicate this book to Caryl Davies and Father Jimmy Thomas; for their friendship, and for sharing their wisdom and knowledge as they nurtured my interest and development in teaching.

Safety across the curriculum

Edited by Carole Raymond

First published 1999 by Falmer Press
11 New Fetter Lane, London EC4P 4EE

Simultaneously published in the USA and Canada
by Falmer Press
Routledge Inc., 29 West 35th Street, New York, NY 10001

Falmer Press is an imprint of the Taylor & Francis Group

Typeset in 10/14pt Melior by Graphicraft Limited, Hong Kong
Printed and bound in Great Britain by TJ International, Padstow

British Library Cataloguing in Publication Data
A catalogue record for this book is available from the British Library

Library of Congress Cataloging in Publication Data
A catalogue record for this book has been requested

ISBN 0 7507 0984 7

Contents

CONTENTS

List of figures

Acknowledgments

During the preparation of this book the authors have consulted many people and numerous publications. The material presented draws together our findings about what we believe is regarded as good practice. We are grateful to the many colleagues and friends for the help and guidance they so willingly offered.

As editor I offer a few individual thank yous to Geoff Edmondson and Kath Keeley whose supportive but critical reviews provided valuable comments and strengthened the manuscript.

I am also grateful to the following for permission to reproduce copyright materials: Tony Bird of the Education and Community Learning section, Northampton County Council, and Dudley Local Education Authority. Also to Geoff Edmondson for providing case reports.

While every effort has been made to acknowledge all sources of information, particularly those bound by copyright, in a few cases this has not been possible and I take this opportunity to offer my apologies to any copyright holder whose right I may have unwittingly infringed.

Introduction

This book offers guidance on the management of safe practice in the primary school. It focuses on key aspects of teachers' responsibilities and selected areas of curriculum provision in the primary school. The purpose is to provide teachers with background knowledge and guidance on safe practice across a range of curriculum areas considered to involve higher levels of risk. It is not a definitive statement of the law nor is it a legal interpretation of any regulations of Act. It offers a selective overview of the responsibilities of teachers and an interpretation of the main legislation and statutory requirements to help teachers approach their daily work with confidence and competence, rather than excessive caution and fear. The discussion offers background information that will help teachers interpret general principles intelligently. Various chapters draw on research evidence, recognised regular and approved practice and the many lessons that can be learned from the accumulated research, experience and wisdom of colleagues.

My interest in this area emanates from my background as a pupil who enjoyed the challenge and risk of both on-site and off-site curricular and extra-curricular activities, and as a teacher of physical education – a subject regarded as a high risk area (Croner, 1987). As a teacher, I was ever conscious that the employment conditions in some schools were woefully inadequate and in some instances put both teachers and pupils at risk. Additionally, my work with both primary and secondary student teachers in Initial Teacher Education has led me to examine much more closely the increasing responsibilities of teachers to secure a safe environment for all. Most recently, like other colleagues, I am increasingly being asked to prepare expert witness reports to be used in cases of negligence. It is evident that Britain is now adopting the North American 'sue mentality' (Lincoln, 1992,

p. 41) and litigious ethos. Litigation is fast becoming big business, with lawyers actively encouraging members of the public who have experienced accident and injury to consider negligence and the pursuit of compensation. This 'compensation culture' has raised the profile of safety through increased consumer awareness and has led to the development of a more systematic approach to the management of safety in schools. The greatest problem is in keeping things in proportion. Stock (1991) believes there is

> ❝ *a very narrow path to be trod between being complacent on one hand and on the other alarmist. Straying in one direction will result in unnecessary disruption and wasted resources, straying in the other direction may result in disaster in one form or another.*   (1991, p. vii)

The book is arranged in two parts. The first, divided into three chapters, provides a general overview of safety requirements. Chapter 1 focuses on the legal, professional and moral responsibilities of teachers necessary to create a framework for safe practice. It covers the duties and requirements placed on teachers, based closely on the wording of the relevant legislation, and offers some insight into the legal process once a charge of negligence is underway. The role of expert witnesses and how they compile a report is discussed. Chapter 2 addresses the preparation and monitoring of policy documents and miscellaneous paperwork that contribute towards developing a safety culture in schools. Whitlam completes this with an overview of risk assessment and the management of risk. Statute and case law examples are used to explain and support the principles being developed.

Part 2 looks at selected high risk areas of the curriculum. These examine a selection of issues and the implications of legislation for policy and practice in these areas. In Chapter 4 Twyford looks at the distinctive features of design and technology and how children are actively engaged in designing and making things. He recognises that if pupils are to realise their potential they need to learn about safety as well as learn in safety. Principles of identifying risk and establishing safety procedures are discussed and illustrated through a ballista project. In the next chapter Taylor examines Information Technology and the increasing need to ensure that both teachers and pupils working with computers are aware of the potential hazards.

The chapter on physical education begins with a look at policy and practice and then moves onto two case reports to determine whether pupil injuries were accidents or a result of negligence. Emerging issues are discussed. Skinner takes us back to the classroom in Chapter 7 and explores some of the safety issues in practical science. He begins with teaching science and the need for a science specific safety policy, and goes on to discuss pupils' responsibilities and how they too must engage in risk assessment and learning to manage their own safety and that of others. The outdoor classroom, a well-used environment for both curricular and extra-curricular activities, is the focus of Chapter 8. Thomas examines the complex interplay of human and environmental factors that differentiates the learning context from that found in the school-based classroom. Drawing on case studies and research incidents, she considers what can be learned from accidents in the outdoors, identifies basic principles of safety and the implications for teachers' practice and pupils' safety in a range of outdoor settings. The concluding chapter provides readers with contact addresses for leading organisations and an overview of selected resource materials to help teachers increase their own understanding of health and safety.

This book is guidance. It should not be treated as a complete and authoritative statement of the law. It is intended to help teachers steer their way through what we believe are the key issues and responsibilities regarding the implementation of health and safety requirements in the classroom. We have deliberately used simple terms to help readers understand some aspects of the law and how it can impact on classroom practice. The exemplar materials illustrated reflect authors' experience of good practice in a variety of contexts. Teaching and learning in the primary school is such a dynamic and unpredictable experience that no one can guarantee that accidents will not happen. We hope this will help readers to do all that is reasonable!

Part one

Chapter 1

Creating a framework for safe practice
Carole Raymond

This chapter will address first, the management of safe practice in the primary school with specific attention to the responsibilities of the class teacher as determined by legislation and case law. Second, it will examine aspects of the litigation process in order to help teachers understand negligence and the role of the expert witness. Finally, two different yet complementary approaches used by teachers to create a safe and effective learning environment for pupils are considered: the management of risk and negligence avoidance (Raymond and Thomas, 1996). As the discussion unfolds, a number of important issues emerge that need to be considered during curriculum planning, classroom practice and the provision of teachers' professional development.

In setting the scene for the discussion it is important to recognise that despite the close management, organisation and supervision of pupils, schools like other social environments are susceptible to accident or risk (Raymond and Thomas, 1996, p. 28). Health and Safety Executive (HSE) statistics (Croner, 1998, Figure 1.1) show that accidents occur in a variety of situations, but that the most hazardous areas include the playground, the sports field and the gymnasium. The Child Accident Prevention Trust (CAPT, 1998) report that nearly 27,000 under 5s and over 350,000 children aged 5–14 were injured in school accidents in the UK in 1995.

A great deal of primary school work involves children in investigation and exploration, often through practical work. Teachers are encouraged to extend and challenge their pupils and offer activities that will involve some risk and thrill. This, coupled with increasing demands for pupils to work independently of the teacher, may involve teachers allowing children greater

FIG 1.1
Major accidents to pupils
in schools

Games and PE	10.9%
Gymnasium	8.9%
Playground	44.5%
Corridors and stairs	9.7%
Classrooms	10.9%
School field	3.8%
Toilets etc.	2.3%
Laboratory	1.9%
Hall	2.9%
Workshops	3.1%
Baths	1.1%

independence and occasionally leaves them feeling more vulnerable. Understanding our responsibilities towards the management of safety is intended to make such learning opportunities safer for young people and teachers. Teaching safely leads to pupils learning safely. While it is recognised that the risk of accident and injury is ever present, the ability to anticipate hazards and to minimise them can be developed early on in a teacher's career. But the management of health and safety, essential to the development of a safety culture, is a shared and collective responsibility that rests not only with the individual teacher, subject teams, the school and its governing body, but also with Local Education Authorities (LEAs), higher education, central government and national associations (TTA, OFSTED, QCA). This is not to ignore the role of pupils in the development of a school safety culture. Since the 1988 Education Act, school governors have assumed increased responsibility for an explicit policy on matters of health and safety and for ensuring that the policy is implemented. In independent and voluntary schools, and schools that have opted out, governors have taken over what was previously the responsibility of the LEA.

It is also important to recognise that sometimes the problems of managing safety can seem overwhelming, but often it is only a matter of formalising procedures that already take place. Others believe it is a matter of common sense. Gold and Szemerenyi (1997, p. 200) remind us that schools do not have an obligation to do the impossible but only to work in a competent and reasonable manner.

Safety has also emerged as a topic in the curriculum to be taught in a number of contexts that are relevant to pupils of all ages. For example, in physical education, science and technology, the curriculum states clearly that pupils must be equipped to recognise hazards and assess risks to themselves and others, as well as the environment. They must also be able to take, suggest or predict appropriate action to control the risks so that they can work safely and in accordance with health and safety requirements. Within information and communication technology, and activities located in the outdoor classroom, there are many places where health and safety issues have relevance and where using different problem-solving and investigative activities, children learn about hazards and risks. Furthermore, they learn how to respond to different situations, thus developing knowledge and understanding of safety in different environments and situations. Through varied experiences teachers must help pupils develop the skills to take responsibility and become response-able. Thus children learn not only to manage their own safety but that of others too.

Teachers' responsibilities

Parliament has given a number of duties to all those involved in education via the Education Acts and a range of powers to enable them to carry out those duties. Safe practice can be planned within this framework of responsibility and duties, beyond which contextual circumstances and a teacher's personal judgment are crucial. The duties of the individual teacher and how they are accountable for their actions is well presented in the case of *Butler v. Cheshire County Council (1996)* where the judgment of His Honour Judge Lachs made specific reference to the PE teacher's sense of responsibility. In an earlier paper, Raymond and Thomas (1996) considered various interpretations of this responsibility and identified three: legal and statutory, professional and moral.

Legal and statutory responsibilities

Over the years, very clear rules and regulations have developed to govern the preparation and supervision of school activities. In fact, education is often considered to be one of the most regulated sections of public life. The law imposes the responsibility for making satisfactory arrangements for health and safety on management, while making provision for safety representatives to monitor their effectiveness. Common law and statute law impose general duties on individuals and bodies.

The framework of common law, which has been built up over many years, is made up of the body of decided law of general applications. This means:

■ the court puts construction on what the legislation means
■ the doctrine of precedent (taking note of previous judgments and the status of the courts which ensures consistency of interpretation. (Croner, 1996, 1–2)

It is not fixed, except by the doctrine of precedent. This requires a lower court to follow a previous judgment of a higher court. The decisions that make up common law include those made in respect of statute law (made by Parliament) on a particular set of facts. Statute law remains superior to common law. If both statute and common law apply in a case, but appear to contradict each other, statute law is followed. However, Parliament can legislate to change or repeal what the common law has established.

In common law there are long-established and important requirements for those acting *in loco parentis* which forms the basis for the *duty of care*. *In loco parentis* is used to describe the responsibility of a teacher towards the pupil and literally means 'in the place of the parent' (Croner, 1992, pp. 3–261). The British Association of Advisers and Lecturers in Physical Education (BAALPE) summarise this as:

> *Teachers and others with this legal responsibility must exercise the same duty of care as would a reasonable parent. In the case of adventurous activities, or at recreational and sports centres, this legal responsibility falls to the accompanying teachers and cannot be delegated to instructors or coaches.*

(BAALPE, 1995, p. 22)

Thus the teacher must behave as a 'reasonable' parent, which over the years has generated much debate about the many different and conflicting attitudes which may be seen as reasonable. The Courts have on many occasions sought to explain reasonableness as common sense, defining the standard of care in a realistic way. In *Hudson v. The Governors of Rotherham School* (1938) Mr Justice Hilbery said:

> *If boys were kept in cotton wool some of them would choke themselves with it. They would manage to have accidents; we always did, we must not always have action at law afterwards.*

> *You have to consider whether or not you would expect a headmaster to exercise such a degree of care that boys could never get into mischief. Has any reasonable parent yet succeeded in exercising such care as to prevent a boy getting into mischief and if he did, what sort of boys would we produce?*

(Croner, 1992, pp. 3–261)

This was reinforced in the case of *Jeffrey v. London County Council (1954)*:

❝ *A balance must be struck between the meticulous supervision of children every moment at school and the desirable object of encouraging sturdy independence as they grow up.*

Clearly the degree of care is not intended to stifle initiative and independence (Croner, 1992, 3–262). It is intended to balance 'robustness', which would make children take the world as they find it, and the 'tenderness' which would give them the care of a nursery whenever their need required it (*Simkiss v. Rhondda Borough Council, 1983*).

The duty of care extends to after-school activities and clubs, off-site activities including schools trips and residential activities (see Thomas, Chapter 8) 'when they are engaged in authorised school activities elsewhere' (DFE/TPCD, 1995, 35.7) and may be 24 hours a day throughout an entire journey. The duty can only be put aside when responsibility is reasonably delegated to others. Additionally, a teacher owes a duty of care where a child is allowed out of school before the end of the day. In the case of *Barnes v. Hampshire County Council (1969)* it was held that the teacher and the LEA were liable as the child was allowed out of school before her mother arrived and was subsequently injured. The judge considered that an accident of this type was foreseeable, as the teacher knew the time the crossing patrol was available. This reminds us of teachers' responsibility for the welfare, upbringing and education of the pupils in their care, in particular, of the need to be constantly mindful for the pupils' health and safety.

Under their authority to act *in loco parentis*, schools have a duty to act independently in respect of Child Protection. This relates to the Children Act 1989 and the duty of a person with care for a child to do all that is reasonable, in the circumstances, to safeguard or promote the child's welfare and protection from harm. Teachers must work with social services departments, the NSPCC and Police whenever they are concerned about a child's safety, in line with procedures adopted by the Area Child Protection Committee (ACPC). The legislation also requires that all persons who come into regular contact or have substantial access to children must provide information as to their suitability. The authority concerned must vet this information. This has enormous implications regarding partnerships and the recent move towards establishing stronger links between a schools and its community, involving a variety of agencies. Some subject areas, for example physical education, have published guidelines for LEAs, schools and colleges in the use of AOTTS (Adults Other Than Teachers) (see BAALPE).

Teachers have a responsibility to know what is reasonable practice. They will undoubtedly be expected to know a great deal more about the propensities of children than a prudent parent. Quite simply:

> if the duty of care is at least as great as that which would be taken by the average, careful parent in the same circumstances then this legal duty is discharged. A prudent parent, of course, would pay due regard to the age, intelligence and physical competence of the child in question.　　　(Stock, 1991, p. 3)

Parents and the general public will inevitably set professional responsibility much higher than that normally expected of a parent and presume that teachers will be more aware of the potential risks for pupils. Add to this recognition that some specialist and complex areas of design and technology, information and communication technology, physical education and science have a higher risk that requires a higher duty of care. As Mr Justice Edmund said in *Lyes v. Middlesex County Council (1962)*:

> I hold that the standard [of care] is that of a reasonably prudent parent judged not in the context of his own home but in that of a school, in other words, a person exhibiting the responsible mental qualities of a prudent parent in the circumstances of school life. School life happily differs from home life.

Establishing the duty of care may also depend upon the specialist knowledge which teachers claim to have or may be reasonably expected to have in the positions which they hold (Croner, 1987, 3–275). This is not to mention the variable class sizes that teachers have to work with.

Under their Conditions of Employment teachers have supervision duties and are required to maintain good order and discipline among pupils and to safeguard their health and safety. This covers all *reasonable steps* to see that children are not exposed to *unacceptable risks* (Croner, 1996, 3–52). This extends risk assessment into practice and covers teachers' ability to observe, monitor and control the learning environment. Teachers are reminded that levels of supervision will need to take into account the nature of the activity, paying particular attention when children are engaged in more dangerous activities with greater risk, using dangerous equipment or handling recognised dangerous substances. Consideration must also be given to the number of children under supervision, age, maturity, ability, previous experience and guidance on what is regular and approved practice.[1]

When pupils engage in activities that carry greater risk, teachers must ensure that pupils are provided with sufficient tuition and supervision to enable them to participate safely. In the cases of *Conrad v. ILEA [1967]* and *Wright v. Cheshire County Council* pupils suffered injuries in classroom activities but no negligence was found as the teachers followed general and approved practice.

All teachers, specialist and generalist, are expected to work within a *modus operandi* which identifies all the foreseeable safety problems associated with activities undertaken in relation to the school curriculum.

Any breach of these duties which cause injury or loss may give rise to a claim for damages (compensation), or sometimes even to criminal penalties. Although accidents will occur because they cannot always be foreseen, teachers have a legal duty to work within a system which demonstrates a realistic use of methods which successfully anticipate and eliminate foreseeable risks. (BAALPE, 1995, p. 21, 1.1.2)

Health and safety legislation

Current Health and Safety legislation has developed from a very piecemeal and badly structured approach at the turn of the century to a rigorous system recommended by *The Robens Report* (1972). This offered a number of recommendations based on a single Act, Health and Safety at Work, to be applied to all places of work. *The Health and Safety at Work Act 1974* (HSW Act) places responsibility on employers (local education authorities, governing bodies, managers of other premises including outdoor centres)[2], and the self employed, to do all that is reasonably practicable to ensure the health and safety of employees (teachers, instructors, coaches and all other staff) and non-employees (pupils and others who enter the school premises, e.g. parents). The degree of responsibility would depend on the extent of the delegated powers, but head teachers in all schools would be considered to have responsibility (NASUWT, 1997).

Most teachers will be familiar with Section 2 (3) of the Act. This places a duty of care on every employer to maintain an up-to-date written statement on general policy in respect of the health and safety at work of employees, and the organisation and arrangements for carrying out that policy (see Chapter 2). Furthermore, this statement must be brought to the notice of employees, and in the case of school, pupils, and relates to safe premises and safe environment. This is particularly important when working off-site, external to the school. The NUT describes the standard of care expected from teachers as 'generally applying skill and awareness of children's problems, need and susceptibilities' (1992, p. 4). In the case of *Butler v. CCC*, the teacher emerged as a caring class teacher who knew her class very well. This may be difficult in some schools where classes can consist of 35 pupils or more, nevertheless, the responsibility remains the same.

The HSW Act also established the Health and Safety Commission with responsibility for publishing specific health and safety regulations and the Health and Safety Executive which enforces the Act by means of an inspectorate with extensive powers that can lead to prosecution. It allows all employees' rights to be represented, meaning that in all schools there will be a designated safety representative who has the right to receive appropriate training and access to information, release from timetable and time out of school to carry out their duties. These include:

- to be consulted by the employer on health and safety matters
- to carry out inspections of the workplace (every three months, after an accident or dangerous occurrence, whenever there is a significant change in conditions or following the publication of new regulations).

The Management of Health and Safety at Work (MHSW) 1992 regulations add to the HSW Act (1974) and spell out the steps employers must take to comply with their health and safety responsibilities. This includes guidelines for risk assessment, thus requiring employers to introduce measures for planning, organising, monitoring and reviewing arrangements for the management of health and safety. This means that school governing bodies and head teachers have a responsibility to identify the levels of risk that exist in curriculum activities and to ensure the design and implementation of effective risk control measures, appropriate systems and policies to manage, control and protect these measures and adequate health and safety training (see Whitlam, Chapter 3, and Thomas, Chapter 8). Griffin (1997) makes an important point when he states:

> *Failure to conduct risk assessments can put a school in breach of the law. Failing to equip pupils with this skill is to miss an opportunity to empower them in relation to their own safety now and in the future.* (1997, p. 3)

Thus risk assessment is not just associated with events, activities and locations, but with children's own personal safety.

First aid arrangements are also an essential part of a school's health and safety policy. This should include arrangements for first aid, numbers of first-aiders/appointed persons, numbers and locations of first aid containers, arrangements for off-site trips, and out-of-school hours arrangements, e.g. lettings, parents evenings (DfEE, 1998, p. 3). Teachers' conditions of employment do not include first aid, although any member of staff may volunteer. Guidance suggests that teachers are expected to use their best endeavours at all times, particularly in emergencies, to secure the welfare of the pupils at the school. A teacher has no duty to administer medication and cannot be required to do so (DfEE, 14/96) but before they do so they must be properly trained. This training could cover how to administer medication safely and how to recognise the symptoms which can lead to medication being required. In all situations it is crucial that the school procedure is followed, in line with clear policy guidelines on medicines, endorsed by procedures for managing medication.

In endeavouring to meet all their health and safety responsibilities, employers must also provide comprehensive information and appropriate training for employees, take account of capabilities when allocating tasks, establish emergency procedures and consult with trade union health and safety representatives. Additionally, *The Workplace (Health, Safety and Welfare) Regulations 1992* require employers to provide reasonable working conditions (heating, lighting, furniture and fittings, cleanliness, sanitary facilities, ventilation, space, floors, rests rooms and so on). *The Education (School Premises) Regulations 1996* derive from the 1944 Education Act and they lay down minimum standards for education premises which cover both the needs for teachers and pupils.

Other new regulations (*Display Screen Equipment, Work Equipment, Personal Protective Equipment*) implement aspects of the MHSW 1992 and *Workplace Regulations* in more detail. These also fulfil some of the European legislation that has shaped our practice since 1993. This relates to the European Community Directives issued by the Council of Ministers under Article 118A of the Treaty of Rome.

The Reporting of Injuries, Diseases and Dangerous Occurrences Regulations 1995 (RIDDOR) applies when major injuries are caused by accidents. This will include accidents resulting in death or major injury, unconsciousness resulting from an electronic shock or lack of oxygen and acute illness caused by pathogen, a substance or infected material, fractures (other than bones in the hands and feet). Dangerous occurrences may be the result of unintentional collapsing or fall of structures (walls, floors or equipment), pressurised vessels exploding, or the accidental release of pathogens which severely threaten health. Reportable diseases could include hepatitis caused by exposure to blood or secretions and occupational asthma resulting from work with epoxy resins or animals. RIDDOR requires that a set of correct procedures for reporting any major accidents are in place and are systematically followed without delay. This requires that all notifiable accidents are reported without delay to the Health and Safety Executive by telephone and, within 10 days, in writing, using the accident report form F2508. Some local authorities provide standardised accident report forms and carry out this function for the schools for which they have responsibility, but many leave it to the individual school. Failure to meet these regulations could lead to prosecution. Some LEAs may require serious/significant accidents to be reported centrally for insurance purposes or as part of their RIDDOR procedures. This process not only fulfils a legal requirement but also provides information that allows authorities to identify where and how risks arise and, if necessary, to investigate serious accidents and advise on preventative action.

The information required needs to include:
- location and time of accident
- name and status of injured party
- names of others involved
- names of witnesses
- nature and site of injury
- details of the activity during which the accident occurred
- circumstances of the accident, including any environmental factors
- protective measures in operation
- training of the injured person for the activity
- the supervision at the time
- any design or facility fault which may have contributed to the accident
- details of treatment at the scene, e.g. attendance by first-aider.

The Control of Substances Hazardous to Health (COSHH) regulations cover the many substances that are used in areas such as science, art and CDT – all of which require risk assessment in terms of how they will be used and the level of risk involved. If a substance is used in different circumstances, then different assessments have to be made. Schools usually subscribe to CLEAPSS (Consortium of Local Education Authorities for the Provision of Science Services) who provide an advice service and offer resources such as 'hazcards' covering all hazardous substances used in normal schools. When making assessments about hazardous substances, it is important that the person responsible is fully aware of the legal requirements, the approved code of practice, and of how and when the product is used. The legal responsibility to ensure that these regulations are met lies with the employer and most LEAs appoint specialist personnel in this area; this may not be the case for independent schools. Where guidance is unavailable, or risk assessments have not been undertaken, it would be prudent for class teachers to adopt their own practices or those common elsewhere in education, e.g. in other schools, LEA and/or professional guidelines, and inform the employer in writing of the action to be taken. It is important to remember that this increase in legal regulation does not guarantee safety and does not always deter providers from taking unacceptable risks or working outside their legal regulations. The important issue for teachers is that they ensure schools address legislation through recognised policy and procedures.

European law

While there appear to be numerous European laws and rulings infiltrating the British legal system, few, at present impinge on school law. At present, UK legislation is required to harmonise with EU law and it is well to keep this in mind and keep abreast of new developments. This is not to say that issues to do with human rights, pupils, parents and teachers, may not be referred to the European Court.

Professional responsibilities

All teachers have a job description that should clearly outline their responsibilities. Subject coordinators will also have some responsibility for health and safety. For example the coordinator has responsibility for:
- raising teachers awareness of regular and approved practice
- making evidence available to illustrate that a reasonable standard of care in terms of planning, organisation and delivery has been provided
- monitoring and evaluation of policy implementation
- helping teachers keep up to date with their duties via additional training
- ensuring policy documents, including risk assessment and accident reports, etc., are available to form an evidence base; curriculum planning, assessment, etc.

Newly qualified teachers must have a knowledge and understanding of health and safety issues (DfEE Circular, 4.98). *The School Teachers' Pay and Conditions Document*, published annually, sets out the professional duties of teachers in England and Wales. An important feature includes:

❝ *maintaining good order and discipline among the pupils and safeguarding their health and safety both when they are authorised to be on the school premises and when they are engaged in authorised school activities elsewhere.*

(1995, par. 35 (7))

This will ensure that teachers are in a position to identify and analyse risks involved in the school curriculum activities and subsequently develop and implement strategies to manage risk and minimise the possibility of accident and injury. According to Sharp (1990), the prime risk areas in school settings seem to be supervision, conduct of the activity and the nature of the activity, and equipment and facilities. While head teachers are expected to maintain adequate systems of supervision to protect all children in the care of the school, this responsibility is delegated to class teachers. The question of what constitutes adequate supervision is dependent on a number of circumstances such as:

- age, maturity, usual standard of behaviour and the number of pupils in question
- the nature of the activity and where it is carried out
- the supervisory ability of the staff.

For example, a teacher might adequately supervise 50 well-behaved pupils on a school field while a ratio of 1 teacher to 5 difficult pupils may be scarcely adequate in the same surroundings. In common law, head teachers are responsible for the system of supervision because they have the detailed knowledge and professional experience necessary to make proper judgments. Proper supervision is concerned with both the quantity and the quality of the supervisor. Thus not only must an adequate number of individuals serve as supervisors, these individuals must be competent to serve in that capacity and to act as reasonable prudent supervisors (Sharp, 1990, p. 3).

Teachers also have responsibility to deliver the National Curriculum Orders and this involves providing an entitlement curriculum for all pupils (DFE, 1995). The Education Act 1993 imposes important responsibilities on the governing bodies of all maintained schools towards children with special educational needs (SEN). This Act requires the Secretary of State to issue, and revise, a Code of Practice giving practical advice on such responsibilities and the governing body must have due regard to this code when carrying out its duties towards all pupils with special educational needs. Failure to do so could lead to negligence in the provision of education.

Another issue, recognised by Whitney (1997), relates to bullying. This follows the news that a school in the London Borough of Richmond agreed an out-of-court settlement with a former pupil in response to his allegations that they had failed to deal with bullying against him. Whitney discusses bullying and raises a number of issues about schools' duty of care to their children as part of their responsibility to protect children from any foreseeable harm. (See also Brierley, 1995.) Clearly the playground and class bully are regarded as serious threats to a potential victim both physically and emotionally.

An area of concern identified by many teachers is that of physical contact with pupils. More and more teachers feel more vulnerable to claims of abuse or over familiarity if they have contact with children. Brierley (1998) considers teaching would be impossible if teachers were prevented from having physical contact with their pupils. He offers a useful overview of what are acceptable and unacceptable forms of physical contact (see Figure 1.2). This advice complements that set out in section 550A of the Education Act 1996, introduced in the Education Act 1997 that came into force in April 1998, which gives explicit power to schools to use reasonable force to restrain pupils, to prevent them, for example, from committing a crime, causing injury to themselves or others, causing damage to property, or causing serious disruption (part 5.3). Reasonable force is open to interpretation and all the circumstances of an intervention would be examined. The provision applies to incidents on the school premises and elsewhere, including school trips, when the member of staff is in charge of the pupils concerned.

FIG 1.2
Physical contact with pupils

Physical contact with pupils:

Acceptable contact – when a distressed pupil needs comfort or reassurance. Offering physical contact in these circumstances is normal and necessary. By contrast, physical contact that is gratuitous, unnecessary and unjustified is not acceptable.

Some teachers come into physical contact with their pupils as part of their teaching duties. There will inevitably need to be physical contact during the process of teaching a pupil a PE exercise or a sporting technique; in a number of PE exercises pupils will need to be physically supported for safety reasons.

Teachers who have first aid responsibilities will need to have physical contact with a pupil who requires first aid.

Unacceptable contact – Some physical contact is unlawful. Touching a child indecently is an offence. Hitting or slapping a child is an assault.

Corporal punishment has been abolished in maintained schools since August 1987, the definition of corporal punishment includes not only use of the cane but other forms of physical chastisement, for example, slapping, rough handling and throwing missiles such as chalk.

Brierley (1998, p. 2)

Whitney (1996) discusses physical contact with pupils in terms of the increasing number of pupils' unsubstantiated allegations of abuse against teachers. He also recognises that a teacher may need to have contact with a child, for example, to put their arm around a troubled child to express sympathy. But he emphasises that any touching must be to meet the child's needs, not the teacher's. He advises that threatening children physically is not acceptable, nor is unwarranted invasion of a child's personal space, especially where gender, culture or religious issues are involved.

Furthermore, it is unwise to box a child in a corner or against a wall or in any way that can be interpreted as a teacher using their body to intimidate. It is clearly important that teachers avoid doing anything which could be misunderstood and endeavour to work within the school's recognised policy and procedures to protect themselves from false allegations.

Teachers' responsibility for ITE – students engaged in school-based training

Since the introduction of school-based training (DFE Circular, 14/93; 9/92), student teachers have spent up to two-thirds of their course time in schools. This has transferred a huge responsibility for training to class teachers. In accepting this responsibility most schools will have engaged in some form of partnership with a local institution of higher education and they will have agreed to provide a training programme enabling schools to meet their new responsibilities. In such partnerships, class teachers will assume the role of teacher-trainer and must recognise the associated responsibilities. Student teachers will expect, and according to their course documentation should receive, constructive guidance with the planning and preparation of materials, teaching methods, management and organisation of both resources and their pupils, and advice on professional conduct. All of these factors will influence and generate safe practice in their teaching. It will be for class teachers to ensure that they prepare trainees to recognise, understand and implement health and safety requirements as laid down by the government at any particular time.

During the training process it is important to recognise that the regular class teacher always retains the duty of care responsibility for the pupils safety and well-being.

Moral responsibilities

Inherent in this professional responsibility is teachers' 'moral' responsibility to ensure that pupils do not feel unreasonably pressurised or coerced during the learning process. Stock (1991) talks about the humanitarian reasons underpinning the need for health and safety in schools. Personal injury can have a severe and life-long impact on a victim's life. In this sense we have a moral duty to each other to avoid such occurrences. Teachers make professional decisions whether a child has the necessary skill, knowledge and confidence to engage in different activities safely. This extends to the pressure and encouragement placed on the child to participate. In some instances children can feel coerced to attempt activities where their anxiety or fear might contribute to an emotionally unrewarding experience or failure to participate safely. This may be interpreted as unreasonable behaviour on the part of the teacher and bring into question the duty of care provided. However, once again there is a very fine line between care for pupils' safety and, on the other hand, making sure they respond to challenge and thereby extend themselves. Making the right decisions undoubtedly draws on a combination of knowledge of pupils, professional knowledge and intuition, shared experience and common sense.

OFSTED has the primary responsibility for monitoring that legal and professional requirements are being met, in particular to examine health and safety practice. During an inspection, inspectors will not only record and report on any aspects observed that in their opinion constitute a threat or risk to health and safety, but also:

- ascertain that the school has a health and safety policy and is aware of statutory requirements and has clear procedures to identify and control risks
- record any irregularities and report them to the head teacher and the employer
- judge whether the school has a responsible attitude towards the education and training of pupils in safe practice.

Any report indicating that schools are failing in certain areas will require immediate action. If this action is not forthcoming, then the Health and Safety Executive may be alerted. As OFSTED reports are public documents, any serious breach of statutory requirements may, in due course, lead to an increase in litigation.

Understanding negligence: guilty or not guilty?

We know that the responsibility for health and safety is important for both pupils and teachers, and it involves maintaining a professional standard of *duty of care*. Schools are generally safe places, but I have already recognised that inevitably accidents still happen. Regardless of safety they are unavoidable and will happen. For example:

- a young lad designing a . . . slipped when using the scissors and cut himself badly . . .
- a young girl fell from the wall bars while climbing during a gymnastics lesson, she broke her ankle . . .
- when working on an experiment a pupil scalded himself . . .

- a pupil slipped on wet leaves on the playground and badly damaged her knee . . .
- a young lad fell caught his foot in a hole on the playing field and broke his ankle . . .

None of these sound unusual accidents, but they do have one thing in common: the LEA was sued for damages and was shown to be liable for the injuries due to negligence. Settlements vary and while the costs are covered for the most part by insurance and public money, litigation is becoming an increasingly costly business. Add to this the intangible costs of damage to staff morale, professional integrity and reputations, staff anxiety and bad publicity. Litigation can be a messy and very costly business.

An analysis of a series of cases reveals the sad fact that many of these accidents and the resulting litigation could have been prevented if the teacher in charge had taken due care as recognised in codes of regular and approved practice. Having established the teachers' responsibilities to provide a duty of care it is essential to recognise that teachers who maintain this through their practice help prevent accidents. Perhaps more importantly, those accidents that do happen should be proven not to have been the result of teacher negligence, wilful or reckless disregard under the duty of care or health and safety legislation. All of this recognises the need for risk management (Chapter 3). This section will examine the early stages of the litigation process and try to help teachers understand negligence, and the role of the expert witness in the legal process of litigation. In doing this it recommends that teachers themselves begin to examine and evaluate their own curriculum practice in the same way. If used effectively, these processes will promote a healthy safety culture in schools that could help reduce the number of successful liability suits. The discussion concludes with a consideration of two different yet complementary approaches to the management of safe practice.

Negligence, insurance and compensation

An injured party can take up to three years from the date of the accident to lodge legal proceedings and claim negligence. This is the beginning of a long process requiring patience and a lot of strength of character. Claims of negligence nowadays are mostly to do with money; what compensation is the injured party due, rather than the pursuit of professional discredit.

Under the laws of vicarious liability, employers are liable for the negligence of the employees who are acting in the course of their employment (Croner,

1993, 3–2). Prior to the 1988 Education Act, the responsibility was placed on LEAs but local management of schools has changed this and in the case of grant maintained, independent and non-maintained special schools and city technology colleges, greater responsibility is directed at the governing body. It is important that teachers know precisely what their responsibility is, to prevent personal liability. Furthermore, they need to be mindful that vicarious liability does not cover acts which occur outside the scope of their employment and personal insurance cover is essential. Gold and Szemerenyi (1997) concluded:

> *The law of negligence, in an oversimplified nutshell, says that everyone owes a duty to take care in relation to those people who can reasonably be foreseen to be at risk from a failure to take such care. There has to be fault on someone's part, that fault has to cause damage to another person, and that person has to be someone who is likely to suffer.* (p. 200)

Furthermore, the damage must be attributable to the negligent act. Any breach of a common law, duty of care or of a statutory duty, which results in injury or loss, may allow the injured person to initiate a claim for damages.

Up until the 1980s the most familiar aspect of negligence related to the duty of care to secure the physical safety of pupils. However, it has become more established that schools have a responsibility in the provision of education (Gold and Szemerenyi, 1997). An example of the latter is where a school has failed to identify a pupil's particular learning difficulties and needs, and whether those involved had exercised the skills that could reasonably have been expected from professionals of their standing with the information at their disposal (p. 200). I have already mentioned Whitney (1997) who drew our attention to the out-of-court settlement by a school in the London Borough of Richmond in response to his allegations that they had failed to deal with bullying against him. The school had little choice but to settle without admitting liability, due to the possible costs that could have been incurred in a lengthy dispute.

To be negligent there has to be a connection between the action of the school and the performance of the pupil. A pupil's claim of negligence against a school, relating to pupil safety on the grounds of negligence, will only succeed if it can be shown that there was negligence on the part of a teacher (or of any other employee) that directly resulted in an injury to a pupil (BAALPE, 1990, p. 16). Negligence is the failure to do what a *reasonable* person would have done in the circumstances, or doing what a *reasonable* person would not have done in the circumstances. Reasonableness is the key word (Croner, 1996, 3–51). Some of the key issues relate to:

- the conditions of the school premises
- safety in the classroom and on the playing field
- first aid and other medical issues
- supervision and instruction – regular and approved practice

Quite often safety is seen as the need to ensure there is no physical danger. The increasing use of the 'outdoor' classroom extends the need to include weather conditions, over exposure to sun and associated consequences.

The burden of proof rests on the plaintiff (the pupil). Negligence must be proved on the balance of probabilities; involving all forms of written evidence, curriculum documents and policies, witness statements, photographs, previous records and accident reports etc. Regular and approved practice develops over time and will influence what courts determine as an acceptable standard of care. The majority of such claims for compensation do not reach court. Nevertheless they are painful experiences for all those involved. Croner (1987) suggests that in cases where negligence is alleged, two questions are asked to establish negligence:

1. Was a duty of care owed to the claimant?
2. Did the person against whom the claim is made fail, either by what he had done or by what he had not done?

Negligence is proven if the answer to both questions is 'yes'. Negligence has to be proved on the 'balance of probabilities', as opposed to the standard of proof required in criminal case of 'beyond reasonable doubt'. It is clear that pure accidents will not support action for negligence and damages. Teachers are not expected to do the impossible, they cannot protect children from every conceivable danger at all times, they are not automatically to blame.

Bramwell (1993, p. 32) offers a further set of questions used to ascertain if the school was negligent:

- Could the accident have been prevented – in other words was the accident foreseeable?
- Was the activity undertaken and the equipment being used appropriate to the age and experience of the children?
- Were the children given adequate warnings about the danger of misusing equipment?
- Did the organisation of the lesson follow normal and accepted practice?
- Did the teacher involved follow/stick to school/LEA policy?
- Did the child received swift and effective attention after the accident?

To establish a case against the school (the teacher) it is necessary to show that a defendant (LEA/County Council) owed the plaintiff (injured party) a duty of care, that the duty had been breached, and that damage had resulted due to that breach. Personal injury does occur in circumstances where no one is legally at fault. In such cases compensation can only be obtained through specific insurance cover. Increasingly schools are encouraging parents to take out personal insurance to cover such eventualities. Teachers would also be wise to take out personal liability via union membership etc.

Reminding ourselves that schools are not expected to do the impossible, but only to work in a competent and reasonable manner and that teachers are not expected to be perfect, they are expected to apply their skills to the standard that is reasonable to expect given their age, experience and general level of qualification. However, if inexperienced teachers perform duties beyond their experience and do so inadequately, the school may be held negligent for damage suffered by pupils as a result of that inadequacy.

Following an accident, parents/guardians who decide to sue will normally have received some free legal advice from a local solicitor. Many solicitors now use local radio, community free newspapers, local and national papers to advertise their services, inviting readers to have a free consultation to determine whether they are eligible for damages. Legal aid and the no win-no fee approach encourage many to pursue negligence in the hope of some form of compensation. Once the decision to proceed is made and the legal wheels are in motion, solicitors acting on behalf of the plaintiff will seek expert opinion. The outcome of such opinion will normally guide the solicitor whether it is appropriate to continue with the proceedings.

The expert witness

Expert witnesses are independent authorities employed to prepare a report on an accident. The expert witness business has evolved in response to the increase in litigation over recent years; so much so that in PE, where it appears most accidents happen, BAALPE have their own Institute of Expert Witnesses. This not only provides a network of contacts and support structures but also offers professional development through a series of training courses organised and delivered by Bond Solon Training. These include excellence in report writing, courtroom skills and cross-examination skills. Expert witnesses are normally colleagues who have an interest in health and safety management, but who are, more importantly, experienced professionals with a depth and breadth of knowledge in particular areas. They not only know, but understand the accepted *modus operandi* and what is accepted in terms of regular and standard practice. They are able to think laterally about the accident identifying key issues. They have 'ideas', they look at the facts and consider all possible arguments and present their material in a way that the uninformed reader will understand. In preparing their report they will have consulted widely and accessed up-to-date legislation before finalising their professional opinion.

In recent years I have trained as an expert witness and have become increasingly involved in the preparation of expert reports. This has helped me to become more familiar with the legal processes but more importantly it has helped me develop a more critical edge to my thinking when planning my own teaching. The whole process has made me keep up-to-date with regular and approved practice, it has made me both keep abreast of my legal and professional responsibilities and consider the moral obligation that I have both to my students and to my colleagues. The latter is particularly important when a teacher is sued for negligence as it has a dramatic effect on the morale of all teachers in the school.

As mentioned earlier, most cases are settled out of court. This is largely because both the defendant and the plaintiff will have involved their own expert witnesses to prepare a detailed report which offers a professional opinion on whether the accident was due to negligence or not.

The expert report

Expert witnesses will inevitably present their reports in different formats. Nevertheless, there are key areas that all experts will address in a systematic way. An example of the key areas are identified in Figure 1.3. It is important to emphasise the need for the report to be impartial and independent, as an expert is providing an opinion based on the facts available. If the evidence presented to expert witnesses is limited, or inconclusive, then it is not unusual for them to request additional information. This might include school policy documents, schemes of work, assessment documents relating to a pupil's level of attainment, SEN statements, maintenance and inspection reports, or to seek answers to specific questions relating to the plaintiff's statement.

A report must paint a picture for the judge and other readers. Presentation must be clear and concise, with complex ideas presented in a way people can understand. Reports must state the obvious. They need to take the reader systematically through the facts; look at all possible arguments and details, conclusions and recommendations. When cases are settled out of court, it is often on the basis of an expert's report. The court will evaluate the expert

FIG 1.3
Expert witness report categories

Expert witness reports are written in a systematic way, and include:

Introduction – this contains the details about the expert witness, his/her credentials and experience.

The **background to the dispute and the issues** – brief details of the people who will be referred to in the report. The assumed or given factual background to the case. This is normally based on the statements available.

The **issues to be addressed** – usually identified by the solicitor.

Technical Enquiry – a factual description of a visit to the site of the accident.

The **facts on which the expert opinion is based** – this involves distinguishing between the facts as seen, as told and those of regular and approved practice. Each issue will be addressed in detail.

The **expert's conclusions** – having considered the evidence, the expert will offer a professional opinion on the accident.

Appendices – details of all material used to support the report.

(Model Report guidelines prepared by the Judicial Committee of the British Academy of Experts)

---

witness and the soundness of his or her wisdom of opinion and the weight to be attached to it. This process is clearly described in the extract from the dicta of Stuart-Smith LJ in *Loveday v. Renton (1990)*:

 This involves an examination of the reasons given for his opinions and the extent to which they are supported by the evidence. The Judge also has to decide what weight to attach to a witness's opinion by examining the internal consistency and logic of his evidence; the care with which he has considered the subject and presented his evidence; his precision and accuracy of thought as demonstrated by his answers; how he responds to searching and informed cross-examination and in particular the extent to which a witness faces up to and accepts the logic of a proposition put in cross-examination or is prepared to concede points which are seen to be correct; the extent to which a witness has conceived an opinion and is reluctant to re-examine it in the light of later evidence, or demonstrates a flexibility of mind which may involve changing or modifying opinions previously held; whether or not a witness is biased or lacks independence . . .

Not all LEAs admit liability but damages are paid to compensate the injured party for pain and suffering. While this sort of conclusion is not entirely satisfactory for the teacher, it does save on the cost and trauma of going into court.

Schools and teachers familiar with the legal process can use the knowledge to guide their own practice in terms of policy and procedures and the development of a safety culture. Bramwell (1993, p. 33) sees much of this as the responsibility of the management team who need to protect their staff by constructing the necessary defences. He suggests these defences are quite simple:

1. Provide in-service training: to include up-to-date definitions of key terms such as *in loco parentis*, '*duty of care*'; an outline of legal responsibilities when caring for children; the opportunity to discuss cases which have gone to court which illustrate the level of risk; and, finally, recommendations for reducing the dangers which are practical and easily administered
2. Establish safety policies: safety policies and curriculum guidelines which clearly express appropriate learning activities, equipment etc.
3. Heighten awareness: health and safety matters should be given a higher profile and shown to be the responsibility of all staff
4. Safety routines: establish and maintain routines that can help predict or prevent hazardous situations arising. All staff should know routines and emergency procedure, which children have medical problems and what to do should they become distressed. How to report new hazards and who to contact
5. Insurance: check that the school has legal liability.

Teachers' cooperation in the management of safe practice is essential. It is often easy to dismiss the need to monitor and improve practice as unnecessary as it won't happen to us. It is in their interest to be more flexible, to cooperate and to at least give consideration to proposed changes and developments.

While accident prevention is the first priority, making sure that there is proper insurance cover comes very close behind. This can be liability insurance and/or personal accident insurance.

■ *Liability insurance*: All teachers employed by the LEA will normally be covered for Third Party Liability insurance to cover their liability. Policies usually indicate guidelines, regulations and restrictions. However, this cover does not extend to activities undertaken outside of the normal requirements of a teacher's duty. It is therefore wise to have additional personal liability cover, for example though a union or professional association.
■ *Personal accident insurance*: LEAs normally cover employees and pupils for death and disablement during the course of school duties.

Additionally, it is common for LEAs and schools to insure all off-site activities (Merlin) and overseas visits. For foreign trips it may be necessary to include personal belongings.

Management of safe practice

Accidents cost money and this can drain already scarce financial resources. Pupils involved in accidents can suffer a variety of pain and trauma, and occasionally these may have life-long consequences. There are also the pressures placed on teachers if accidents result in the threat of legal action and the pursuit of proof of negligence and compensation. This, coupled with an increase in litigation, legislation and more structured teacher responsibilities, has led to a more formal approach to the management of safety in schools. The level of risk can be reduced and managed if it is recognised. We have already looked at the first stage in this process by establishing and trying to understand the full range of responsibilities. The next stage is to extend this understanding and awareness of the different approaches to meeting and fulfilling these responsibilities; much of this relies on understanding why accidents happen.

Understanding why accidents happen

Understanding and dealing with 'hazards' tends to dominate much of the literature on safety, but as Jones and Lane (1996, p. 2) comment: 'Hazards alone do not cause accidents. A hazard often needs to be combined with an unsafe action to cause an accident'. Thomas (1994) examined a number of case studies and suggested there were a number of similarities contributing to why accidents happen:

- 'Bad luck' factors outside the teachers' control
- Poor decision making and subsequent reaction to the situation
- Lack of adequate and appropriate group management, supervision and organisation
- The over-estimation of
  (a) the teacher's ability/knowledge, understanding and competence
  (b) the pupil's sense of responsibility
- The under-estimation of potential risk and hazard.

Gold and Szemerenyi (1997) recognise the difficulties facing all those who work with children, when they state that the problem is that children are endlessly inventive, and the ways in which an accident can arise are limitless. If we add to this the recognition that most children are unpredictable and do not always behave as expected, accidents will continue to happen. But apart from these elements outside of our control and bad luck, there is much we can do to avoid accidents. We can clearly examine and learn from the accidents, experiences and, mistakes and good practice of others. In doing this we recognise the importance of reality and how it can be used to develop teachers' awareness through in-service training and thereby inform future practice.

There are various approaches to the management of safety, the two most commonly found in schools are risk management and negligence avoidance. *Risk management* requires a careful evaluation of general practice and specific activities, the potential hazards and what could happen to pupils, teachers or others in the teaching and learning environment. This has been described as a formal process of assessing exposure to risk and taking whatever action is required (The National Association of Independent Schools, 1988). Both Sharp (1990) and Bramwell (1993) when discussing negligence and risk management refer to the best approach as one that involves preventative action. Since the *Management of Health and Safety at Work Regulations* (1992) risk assessment (RA) has become a legal requirement and is an employer's responsibility, although the task of assessing the risks will normally be delegated to employees. It is for the employer to lay down the requirements and duties, and for the governors, head teacher and teachers to comply with them.

RA is a thinking process, it involves teachers consulting the school's general risk assessments and acting upon them. Risk assessments are carried out in different ways (see Whitlam Chapter 3, Thomas Chapter 8, Jones and Lane (1997), and Griffin (1996)) and regardless of the approach adopted, they provide a structure within which to satisfy organisational and management responsibilities under health and safety law, the national curriculum, and OFSTED. Croner (pp. 3–76, 1995) suggests the employer must weigh-up the seriousness of any potential hazard against the practical problems and costs of attempting to remove it. If a particular risk is so significant that it cannot be ignored, then the employer need take no more action. Even if the risk is more than insignificant, it may be that practical difficulties, and the costs involved in addressing that risk are so great that it would not be reasonably practicable to take those steps. However, there may be some cases where although the costs are great, so is the risk and it is, therefore, reasonable to expect the employer to incur those costs.

The risk assessment process involves not only teachers, but also pupils. Griffin (p. 4, 1996) rightly recognises it is about 'Educating children and young people in the principles and techniques of conducting risk assessment which will equip them with a skill which is not only transferable to a variety of educational activities, but even more importantly, a skill essential for life'.

Negligence avoidance involves many of the processes involved in risk management but the crucial difference is that the teacher's primary concern is with the prevention of litigation and protection of the self, school and the LEA. In this approach the teacher sees pupils and parents as potential claimants and adversaries. There is emerging evidence that teachers are

> *changing curriculum and extra-curricular provision – removing more challenging activities where the perceived risk of legal action in the case of an accident outweighs the educational benefits; and relying on characteristically safe and more traditional teaching styles involving inflexible methods of discipline, thus endeavouring to reduce the potential for misbehaviour and accident.*
>
> (Raymond and Thomas, forthcoming)

Other authors believe that as British and European society becomes more aware of legal rights and issues of entitlement, and cases of negligence increase, so negligence avoidance will become the more dominant approach (Laurence, 1988; Gray, 1995).

Whatever approach is adopted, it will clearly impact upon the curriculum in different ways. Managing safety requires not an either/or approach, but a synthesis of the two approaches. Perhaps developing teachers' understanding of regular and approved practice, the concept of negligence and the evidence on which a decision is made will help shape future policy and the management of safe practice.

Notes

1. Expert bodies that offer detailed guidance: Association for Science Education; The National Association of Advisers and Inspectors in Design and Technology; The British Association of Advisers and Lecturers in Physical Education; Plus DES and DFE publications *Safety in Science*.
2. In a school context the employer is the LEA in county, controlled and special agreement schools, and in pupil referral units; the governing body is the employee in CTC, voluntary aided, non-maintained special, grant-maintained and grant-maintained special schools; the owner or the trustee is the employer in some independent schools.

References

BAALPE (1990) *Safe Practice in Physical Education*, Leeds: White Line Press.

BAALPE (1995) *Safe Practice in Physical Education*, Dudley: Dudley LEA.

BARRELL, G. R. and PARTINGTON, J. A. (1985) *Teachers and the Law*, 6th edn., Cambridge: Methuen.

BRAMWELL, A. (1993) 'A cautionary tale of negligence', *Management of Education*, **7**, 1, Spring.

BRIERLEY, D. (1995) 'Bullying', *Croner Teacher's Briefing the Teacher's Legal Guide*, **24**, May.

BRIERLEY, D. (1998) 'Physical contact with pupils', *Croner Teacher's Briefing the Teacher's Legal Guide*, **54**, February.

CAPT (1998) *Lessons for Safety. Teacher's Guide for Key Stages 1 and 2*, Child Safety Week Resource Pack.

CRONER (1987) *The Head's Legal Guide*, Kingston-upon-Thames: Croner Publications.

CRONER (1986–98) *The Head's Legal Guide – In loco parentis.* Loose-leaf document, Kingston-upon-Thames: Croner Publications.

DFE (1992) *Initial Teacher Training (Secondary Phase)*, (Circular 9/92), London: HMSO.

DFE (1993) *Initial Teacher Training (Primary Phase)*, (Circular 14/93), London: HMSO.

DFE (1995) *Physical Education in the National Curriculum*, Revised Orders, London: HMSO.

DFE (1995) *Teachers' Pay and Conditions*, London: HMSO.

DfEE (1996) *Supporting Pupils with Medical Needs in Schools*, Circular 14/96.

DfEE (1998a) *Guidance on First Aid for Schools: A Good Practice Guide*, London: HMSO.

DfEE (1998b) *Teaching: High Status, High Standards. Requirements for Courses of Initial Teacher Training*, Circular 4/98, HMSO.

GOLD, R. and SZEMERENYI, S. (1997) *Running a School: Legal Duties and Responsibilities; 1998*, Bristol: Jordans.

GRAY, G. R. (1995) *Safety Tips from the Expert Witness*, JOPHERD, January.

GIFIS, S. H. (1975) *Law Dictionary*, New York: Barrons.

GRIFFIN, M. (1996) 'Risk assessment for pupils and schools', *The Head's Legal Guide Bulletin*, **29**, July.

HMSO (1974) *Health and Safety at Work Act*, London: HMSO.

HMSO (1992) *The Management of Health and Safety Regulations*, London: HMSO.

HMSO (1994) *The Control of Substances Hazardous to Health*, London: HMSO.

HMSO (1995) *The Reporting of Injuries, Disease and Dangerous Occurrences Regulations*, London: HMSO (RIDDOR).

JONES, L. and LANE, M. (1997) *Together Safely*, Safer Pupils Resource Pack, London: University of Greenwich.

LAURENCE, M. (1988) 'Approaches to safety management part 1', *Canadian Association for Health, PE and Recreation*, **54**, 4, pp. 13–17.

NATIONAL ASSOCIATION OF INDEPENDENT SCHOOLS (1988) *Risk Management for Schools*, Boston.

NATIONAL ASSOCIATION OF SCHOOLTEACHERS AND UNION OF WOMEN TEACHERS (NASUWT) (1997).

NATIONAL UNION OF TEACHERS (1992) 'Beyond the classroom', *Guidance from the NUT on School Visits and Journeys*, NUT.

OFSTED (1997) *School Inspection: A guide to the law*, November *1997*.

RAYMOND, C. W. and THOMAS, S. M. (1996) 'Safe practice: Teachers' responsibilities regarding risk', *Journal of Teacher Development*, **5**, 1, February, pp. 27–32.

RAYMOND, C. W. and THOMAS, S. M. (forthcoming) *Health and Safety Legislation: Teachers' Current Practice and Anxieties in Physical Education*.

ROBENS REPORT (1972) *Safety and Health at Work*.

SHARP, L. (1990) *Sport Law*, NOLPE.

STOCK, B. (1991) *Health and Safety in Schools*, Kingston-upon-Thames: Croner Publications.

THOMAS, S. M. (1994) 'Adventure education: risk and safety out of school', *Perspectives*, 50, University of Exeter School of Education.

WHITNEY, B. (1997) 'Dealing with Bullying', *The Head's Legal Guide Bulletin*, 26 January.

Legal case studies

Barren v. Hampshire County Coucil (1993)

Butler v. Cheshire County Council (1996)

Lyes v. Middlesex County Council (1962) 61 LGR 443; LTG 198

Jeffrey v. London County Council (1954) 52 LGR 21

Hudson v. The Governors of Rotherham School (1938) LCT 302

Stuart-Smith LJ in Loveday v. Renton (1990)

Chapter 2

Policy and paperwork
Carole Raymond

In today's climate of accountability it is essential that teachers' paperwork serves to provide a solid *evidence* base for anyone wanting to examine their practice (parents, governors, inspectors, the court) and should be given due priority. For many, the hardest part of any paperwork is getting started. Someone once gave me good advice, 'Don't get it right, get it written. You can then start to make it right.' Once a first draft is ready, consultation and discussion with staff will help refine documents and make them working documents. This way of shaping any paperwork will also help develop staff ownership and a sense of openness, thus promoting a 'togetherness' in safety management. Furthermore, it recognises that the development of a safety culture is the responsibility of everyone in school, including pupils.

In establishing a framework for safe practice, paperwork refers to

- **Whole school policy:** the school's intentions towards the management of health and safety
- **Curriculum guidelines:** general and specific, how policies are integrated into teaching and learning, planning of schemes of work, units of work and lesson plans
- **Miscellaneous documents:** pupil assessment records, accident reports, teachers' lesson notes, pupil records of attainment and attendance, maintenance reports etc.
- **Quality assurance:** review and evaluation of school policies

Such well-defined documentation should reflect a well-managed system, that reduces risk, empowers people to take action and ensures that people discharge their responsibilities effectively. It will establish common codes of practice, common administrative procedures and begin to ensure those statutory requirements and other national guidelines such as codes of practice are followed.

Whole school policy statements

The Health and Safety Executive recommend that employers should devise their own policy statement in cooperation with school management teams and other employees. An adopted policy, for example, *Be Safe!* (ASE, 1990) in science or *Safe Practice in Physical Education* (BAALPE, 1996), might not reflect the individual circumstances of each school. However, some LEAs might insist that their policy statements should be used, in which case it is recommended that schools annotate such documents and/or add appendices to prescribed guidelines that specify the needs of the school.

There is endless guidance on drawing up whole school policy statements (Harrison, 1995a, 1995b) and LEAs usually provide exemplars. But specific health and safety guidance is given by *Safety Policies in Education and the Education Sector* (revised edition, 1994), *The Responsibility of School Governors for Health and Safety* (third impression, 1993) and *Health and Safety Management in Schools* (1995). Croner (1997, 3–9) offers some simple guidance:

- State the commitment of the school's management to safeguarding health and safety
- Identify which personnel are responsible for the various aspects of the policy
- Clearly describe the procedures put in place
- Involve all staff and provide for them to be informed and trained
- Ensure that the procedures for safeguarding health and safety are monitored.

It is important therefore that it:
- outlines a statement of 'intent', the purpose, 'why it is needed' as well as what has to be done
- is presented in a straightforward style
- uses language that is suitable for all
- has clear arrangements about what people 'should' do [urge/wish] and what people 'must' [required to] do
- has clear details about expected level of performance, e.g. weekly, monthly, annually
- is copied to all staff.

Evidence has to be as thorough as possible. It is therefore recommended that the following key areas be addressed in a safety policy:

- *The purpose*: this creates the 'ethos' and is the basis of developing a 'safety culture'. It must state what is to be provided generally and more specifically in relation to teaching and learning.
- *Accidents*: how they are to be handled, notification of parents, investigations, etc.
- *First Aid*: identify first-aiders and specify where first aid boxes are located.
- *Fire Precautions*: drills, maintenance of exit routes, regular maintenance.
- *Hazards*: risk assessments/responsibilities and procedures (see Chapter 3 for further details).
- *Environment*: identification of defects, maintenance and repair.
- *Electrical safety*: equipment, maintenance and inspection.
- *Substances*: handling and storage.
- *Infectious diseases*: information, necessary precautions.
- *Safety representatives and safety committee*: names, structure and responsibility.
- *Inspections* (site facilities): frequency, records – audit checklists (see exemplar Appendix 1).
- *Information*: details of advice available, how staff can access health and safety information.
- *Staff*: communication about information, training and ongoing professional development.
- *New staff*: how and when they can be briefed about school arrangements.
- *Curriculum guidelines*: schemes of work, assessment arrangements.
- *Pupils*: management of pupils, procedures, discipline.

All class teachers and coordinators need to be familiar with the school policy contents and procedures and link the school aims with curriculum-specific policy statements. This will create an appreciation of the 'wholeness' of health and safety management. It will also help to ensure that class teachers, at the heart of the teaching and learning proces, are well informed with expected practice. Similarly, school management, governors and head teachers, will need to ensure needs arising out of health and safety policies feature as priority items in the school development plan.

In many ways the management of safe practice is seen as common sense. However, common sense for teachers is reliant on an existing body of professional knowledge, that is perhaps no different to what is often recognised as 'standard', 'normal' or 'approved' practice. This refers to what has built up over the years as teachers established and regularly used practice and procedures that have reliably avoided foreseeable accidents without reducing the challenge and developmental value of the subject for young people (BAALPE, 1995, p. 23).

Curriculum guidelines

Curriculum guidelines refer to how different subjects and topics are taught and the selection and order of material throughout a particular Key Stage. They should address and develop a number of main issues identified in the school subject safety policy. A useful framework is outlined below.

Rationale	Purposes of teaching the subject/topic Its contribution to the curriculum Its relevance for pupils now and in the future Statutory requirements which need to be met How it contributes to the school aims
Teacher	Preparation Discipline/rewards procedures Attitude/role model Supervision, class management, discipline and order
Pupils	Behaviour expectations Clothing, footwear (personal protection) Jewellery
Lesson structure	Content Progression Organisation (pupils, equipment) Evaluation
Facilities	On-site – inside, outside Off-site/community links
Apparatus	Organisation layout Safe handling, storage
Special educational needs	Requirements for different subjects: Adapt/modify activities/apparatus
Medical conditions	Pupils with medical conditions, sick notes
Accidents	Procedures, First Aid
Special areas	Swimming pools/gymnasium/playground: arrangements, guidelines, special instructions
Assessment	Record keeping, checklist regarding safety
Special features	Risk assessments/fieldwork policies/special procedures, e.g. absence, additional support

Schemes of work provide details of teachers' long-term planning for pupils' learning and should set out a series of units of work relating to different activities or topics. From this teachers should plan their lessons according to individual class and pupil needs. The scheme should cover

- an overview to show progression, continuity and the relationship between units of work
- a plan, including timescale, for each Key Stage and each year group.

Each unit of work should provide a clear focus on:
- Learning objectives
- Content – programmes of study, attainment targets
- Time available and distribution
- Pupil activities and experiences
- Resources available
- Assessment opportunities
- Provision for different abilities, cross-curricular links, ICT, homework, advice on teaching styles and any special features regarding health and safety.

In science and design technology this may include reference to codes of conduct when using different pieces of equipment, movements around the work space, when working in groups, etc; or in physical education, the need to warm up before any vigorous activity, safe exercise; or in ICT the need to check posture and avoid sitting at VDUs for extensive periods of time.

Miscellaneous documents

Accident reports, teachers' lesson notes, pupil records of attainment and attendance, maintenance and audit reports, etc.

Anyone entering a school building and special work areas will feel the atmosphere of the school or subject ethos. For example, when you walk into a primary classroom the wall displays, the behaviour of the pupils, the relationship between pupils and teacher all make up the culture of the school. If this embraces 'safety' then posters/notices around the school reminding pupils of the need to *Be Safe*, provide good evidence that the school is endeavouring to promote a safety culture.

Teachers usually have lesson plans and notes that briefly record the content of their lessons. These are useful records should a teacher be alleged to be negligent. Similarly, pupil records and registers provide evidence of attainment and attendance in cases where supervision is questioned and the appropriateness of activities, continuity and progression, etc.

Raymond and Thomas (forthcoming) research evidence suggests that schools have procedures for accidents. These refer to 'accidents, how to deal with reports, etc.' as key aspects of the health and safety policy. Croner (1986, 3–288) suggests that all but obviously minor injuries to children should be recorded in writing with a brief statement of how the injury occurred, as soon as possible after the incident while memories are still clear and fresh. The supervision arrangements in force at the time should be noted. The recording of details is particularly important where issues of contributory negligence may arise. It is important that the reports are checked and make reference to fact rather than opinion. Should a case proceed to court, these statements are crucial items of evidence. An exemplar is provided in Figure 2.1.

If teachers are to manage safety in a proactive way, it is important that they can answer 'yes' to the following questions:

- Have you written emergency procedure?
- Is the procedure known to all and posted clearly throughout the school?
- Who are the qualified first-aiders?
- What happens if an accident/injury occurs in a classroom/playground/ gymnasium/playing field?
- Have you prepared and published the emergency procedure for visits to off-site venues? (swimming pool/other schools/activity holidays, etc.)
- What is the emergency contact strategy? For example: How do you contact the injured parties' parents?
- When do you practise these strategies?
- Do you record when you practise them?

Parent/guardian consent forms for educational visits and overnight stays

Schools offer a vast range of both curricular and extra-curricular experiences for pupils (especially in relation to science and physical education) that take pupils into what is recognised as the outdoor classroom. In Chapter 8, Thomas discusses many of the specific health and safety requirements which shape these experiences. It is crucial that parents are informed about the exact nature of the experiences to be offered, furthermore they need to be involved in educating their children about the special codes of conduct that may be required. Teachers will therefore have to send out a parent/guardian consent form (see Figure 2.2) and a code of conduct contract.

Injured or affected person

Surname:	Forename(s):	
Address:	Age:	Gender:
	Status:	
	Tutorial if student:	

Details of accident or incident

Nature (state whether injury, near miss or other):	
Location:	
Date:	Time:
Witnesses:	

Details of injury

Nature (if none write none):					
Part of body:					
Treatment (tick boxes):					
No treatment	☐	First Aid	☐	Resumed work/ returned to class	☐
Sent home	☐	Attended GP	☐	Sent to hospital	☐
Parent/Carer contact successful/unsuccessful	☐	Time	☐	Detained for ___ hours	☐

Outcome

Not off work or school	☐	Off work or school more than 3 days	☐	Permanent partial disability	☐
Off work or school less than 3 days	☐	Permanent total disability	☐	Temporary incapacity	☐

Description of events leading up to accident or incident

FIG 2.1
School accident report

Description of immediate actions

Description of possible causes

Description of possible causes

Review of options to prevent re-occurrence

Recommendations

Report completed by

| Name: | Signature: | Date: |

FIG 2.1
Cont'd

FIG 2.2
Parental consent form

Parental/guardian consent form needs to feature
The nature and purpose of the visit
Emergency details – including an agreement that the child can receive medical treatment, etc.
Medical information
Insurance cover
Declaration of understanding and permission granted
Form to be signed and returned to the school.

Special codes of conduct for pupils on educational visit also need to be issued along with the consent form. These make reference to:

■ Behaviour expectations
■ Declaration that the parent has discussed these with their child.

Other useful documents that promote a safety culture include formal audits of health and safety in specific high risk areas. The checklist in the Appendix (p. 157) is an example of such an audit in physical education. The different sections serve as a reminder to both teachers and coordinators of the many aspects of health and safety and the completed pro forma is a useful document to be used to shape a subject development plan and may even identify teachers' inservice training needs.

Quality assurance: review and evaluation of school policies

If we acknowledge that paperwork is onerous, it is perhaps easy to leave it, even ignore it, once it is done. Approved practice means that policies and practice are regularly monitored, evaluated and reviewed. It is important that all paperwork is dated and this will provide evidence that documents are updated. Accident reports are excellent sources of evidence during an evaluation/exercise, but reports are often filed and left untouched following an accident. It appears that very few schools analyse these reports and discuss whether the:

■ Accident could/should have been avoided with reasonably practicable arrangements
■ The necessary action was taken as quickly as possible
■ The member of staff responsible at the time consulted as to whether any improvement can be implemented. (Croner, 3–21)

This information should be used during risk assessment and the identification of hazards.

Developments in practice and legislation are continuous in education. It is important that those with delegated responsibilities for health and safety keep abreast of changes via professional associations and communicate these to all concerned. When documents are updated it is important to record the time and ensure that staff are circulated with updated copies. Good communication is the prerequisite for effective management regardless of the approach. It is not enough to provide information, both the experienced and the inexperienced teacher need to be trained and observed. As knowledge develops so teachers need opportunities to be updated and have skills revised. This can involve

- news bulletins posted in staff post boxes or on staff notice boards
- discussions at staff meetings
- safety specific staff development.

Pupils, too, need to be taught about safety and depends on the class teacher being prepared to integrate learning about safety in the opportunities they provide for pupils. This requires evaluating and refining classroom practice as part of an ongoing process, integral to creating an effective teaching and learning environment.

References

ASE (ASSOCIATION FOR SCIENCE EDUCATION) (1990) *Be Safe! Some Aspects of Safety in School Science and Technology for Key Stages 1 and 2*, 2nd edn., Hatfield: Association for Science Education.

BAALPE (1996) *Safe Practice in Physical Education*, Dudley: White Line Press.

CRONER (1986–98) *The Head's Legal Guide – In loco parentis*, Kingston-upon-Thames: Croner Publications.

HARRISON, M. (1995a) 'Developing a Key Stage 1 policy for your subject area', in DAVIES, J. (ed.) *Developing a Leadership Role in Key Stage 1 Curriculum*, London: Falmer Press.

HARRISON, M. (1995b) 'Developing a Key Stage 2 policy for your subject', in HARRISON, D. (ed.) *Developing a Leadership Role in Key Stage 2 Curriculum*, London: Falmer Press.

NORTHAMPTONSHIRE EDUCATION AND COMMUNITY LEARNING (1998) *Physical Education Health and Safety Audit – Checklist*, Unpublished resource.

RAYMOND, C. W. and THOMAS, S. M. (forthcoming)

Chapter 3   Risk assessment and the management of risk
Peter Whitlam

Many head teachers and teachers express concern about their health and safety responsibilities. This may be due partly to occasional tragedies such as the Dunblane and Lyme Bay incidents, partly due to an awareness of the developing poor physical state of many schools (OFSTED, 1998) and partly due to a feeling of ignorance about the relevant legislation. This chapter seeks to provide a general overview of risk assessment within the current legal framework and to explain the practical process of managing risk within the curriculum. Statute and case law examples are used to explain and support the principles being developed.

Health and safety is an integral aspect of management for legal, humanitarian and economic reasons. The Local Educational Authority (LEA), or governing body in foundation schools, has ultimate responsibility for safety. School governing bodies apply the LEA's responsibility through committees and/or the head teachers who are responsible for everything over which they have control. Where head teachers do not have control, such as with capital expenditure to eliminate a hazard, they are expected to take all reasonable measures to minimise a problem. Subject leaders are responsible to the head teacher for health and safety issues within a curriculum area, as part of their management responsibility. Class teachers are responsible for the immediate areas of their work and are expected to take all reasonable steps to eliminate risks and to report any safety matters to senior management – for example, to report that a piece of equipment is broken or that a floor is wet and slippery. They must ensure that the pupils are not put at risk because of the hazard. These responsibilities cannot be delegated but the tasks necessary to discharge the responsibility may be delegated where appropriate. In summary, the governors and head teachers must ensure that health and safety policy, including risk management, is implemented; teaching staff usually carry out the task.

Most schools' staff have long carried out informal safety checks on a day-to-day basis and have involved pupils in safety education through posters, units of work and questioning about safe practice – they have taught safely and taught safety. There is also, however, an absolute duty on employers, the LEA or governing body, to carry out a formal, systematic examination of the premises, equipment and work activities – a task usually delegated to those on-site. Awareness of this responsibility by teachers is increasing but is applied variably. It is important that individual teachers as classroom, subject and phase managers recognise and apply their management responsibilities in health and safety, ensuring that safety issues are regularly checked. Those with management responsibility at all levels should know the principal risks associated with their areas of responsibility together with the procedures necessary to minimise the risks.

Everyone carries a legal duty of care, established as the 'neighbour principle'. In The Donoghue case (1932) it was said that 'neighbour' means anyone so closely and directly affected by someone's act or omission that they ought reasonably to have been considered. This duty seeks to ensure that a person takes reasonable care in a situation in which loss or injury to someone else could be anticipated. It is universally recognised that teachers owe a duty of care to pupils and any harm would need to arise from a failure in that duty (see also Chapter 1). This is the concept of negligence – sometimes described as carelessness.

The teacher's duty of care has for many years been set at the standard of a prudent parent described by the phrase '*in loco parentis*', as established in *Williams v. Eady (1893)*. This standard was later modified to be judged in the context of the school where a teacher has responsibility for more pupils than a parent would have at home (*Lyes v. MCC, 1962*). Duty of care is thus judged as the standard expected of a reasonable person to show the level of competence associated with the proper discharge of professional duties. This has been described as the standard reasonably expected of a person in a particular post such as that of a class teacher (*Wilsher v. EHA, 1986*). It is important to remember that the law requires less experienced professionals to be judged at the same standard as more experienced colleagues to avoid inexperience being used as an excuse in negligence. However, the standard of care expected does increase with experience and specialist expertise – described by Denning L J as 'the standard goes up as men become wiser' (*Qualcast Ltd v. Jaynes, 1959*). This is sometimes referred to as a higher duty of care where a teacher, through training or experience such as that in being a subject coordinator or specialist, may be expected to visualise more clearly the results of his or her actions in specialist areas.

The degree of risk involved in an activity or situation influences the decision as to whether a breach of duty of care has occurred. Risks which are reasonably likely to happen should have been anticipated (*Bolton v. Stone, 1951*). However, progressive and appropriate pupil responsibility as they become more mature, experienced and independent is acceptable (*Jeffrey v. LCC, 1954*). Situations carrying intrinsically greater risks such as outdoor activities, contact sports, complex technological equipment and some scientific processes are acceptable provided that appropriate experience, careful preparation and sound teaching have significantly reduced the level of risk. This exercise of due care was accepted in the Van Oppen (1989) case in which a pupil was seriously injured in a game of rugby but it was judged that proper tuition had taken place. This indicates that although various educational activities carry risks they need not be avoided for this reason alone. Risks need to be minimised to ensure that an activity is carried out in a safe manner by guarding against any reasonably foreseeable event. Teachers must therefore take a range of factors into account before allowing an activity or situation to occur. These would include consideration of age, type of activity, previous experience, level of supervision, suitability of equipment or apparatus and using common and approved practice.

As well as the issue of duty of care in relation to risk, a teacher's work is influenced by a range of statute law the principles of which are not always well known. The 1974 Health and Safety at Work Act is based on a principle of accident prevention. It seeks to secure the health, safety and welfare of those at work and to protect others against health and safety risks arising from the activities of those at work. It establishes liability for creating or allowing any situation that might foreseeably cause injury and failing to provide protection against the hazard.

The Act places a duty on employers (the LEA, board of governors, trustees etc.) to provide
- safe plant, work places and systems of work
- arrangements for the safe handling, transport and storing of substances and articles which may be a risk to health
- information, instruction, training and storing of substances and articles which may be a risk to health
- information, instruction, training and supervision to ensure the health and safety of employees.

Employees (teachers and non-teaching staff) must take reasonable care for their own safety and that of others who may be affected by their acts and omissions at work. This places a responsibility on teachers for pupils and other visitors to the school. Employees must also cooperate with an employer in relation to the employer's duties for health and safety. This legislation requires schools to have

- a written policy for health and safety
- the organisation to implement the policy – including some reference to risk assessment and risk control
- arrangements to inform staff of the ways in which the policy is put into practice – such as procedures to be followed and guidance on carrying out risk management.

In addition, the Occupiers Liability Acts, 1957 and 1984, impose a duty of care on the occupier of premises – that is the person or body in control of the premises – for the safety of visitors. This requires measures to be taken to ensure that lawful visitors are safe when using the premises for the agreed purpose of the visit. Teachers must thus ensure that they and the pupils, as visitors, work within a safe environment during their lessons and other sanctioned activities by reporting any faults to the head teacher so that the governing body or LEA, as 'occupiers', may take action.

The Health and Safety at Work Act is enforced by a series of official Regulations or Statutory Instruments such as the *Control of Substances Hazardous to Health (COSHH) Regulations*, 1988, and the *Management of Health and Safety at Work Regulations, 1992*. These are further supported by Approved Codes of Practice (ACOPs) which are not law but guidance provided by bodies such as the Health and Safety Executive or Department for Education and Employment which would be used as the yardstick for the standard of care expected. The COSHH Regulations require the formal assessment of risks that may arise from the use of substances deemed to be hazardous to health and the implementation of specified precautions relating to storage, use, practices and protective equipment. Periodic formal inspection and the maintenance of records are also required. While numerous substances used in science, design and technology and art are used in schools in particular circumstances, following the required procedures is made easier by the use of 'Hazcards' provided by the Consortium of Local Education Authorities for the provision of Science Services (CLEAPS). Hazcards, used in conjunction with schemes of work are deemed to constitute suitable and sufficient assessments by the Education Safety Advisory Committee (ESAC) for Science and Design and Technology.

The Management of Health and Safety Regulations, 1992 (MHSWR) ensures that the principles of the Health and Safety at Work Act are put into practice by setting out general health and safety duties on employers – particularly a requirement to carry out risk assessments. Employees – i.e. teachers and support staff – are also required to act in accordance with safety instructions and training and to report situations which present hazards to health and safety. The MHSWR impacts not only on the application of the Health and Safety at Work Act and subsequent possible criminal liability but also on the civil liability of negligence. This is because the regulations set out not only specific legal standards, but also set acceptable standards for safe practice that could if not met represent a breach of duty in negligence. The requirement for risk assessments may be of considerable significance when considering the extent to which a teacher charged with negligence had shown forethought in planning.

The 1992 regulations require a suitable and sufficient assessment of all the health and safety risks to put in place appropriate arrangements to protect people's health and safety. Risk assessments, then, are simply systematic general examinations of the activities, environment and procedures which will enable those responsible to identify the risks posed by working methods, processes, equipment and environmental influences. This involves:

■ identifying significant hazards which have the potential to cause harm
■ determining the degree of risk posed by the hazards by estimating the severity and likelihood of harm occurring
■ setting out the action required to minimise or eliminate the risks.

A more detailed checklist of aspects to consider when conducting a risk assessment are outlined in Figure 3.1. In practice this is simply part of the planning, preparation and presentation good teachers have done for years.

Confusion may arise from the use of different terminology. Risk assessment is a term used widely as a loose description for the process of managing risk. Risk assessment, risk management and risk control are sometimes used interchangeably.

■ 'Risk management' should be the umbrella term given to the whole process of identifying risks and then taking action to eliminate them.
■ 'Risk assessment' should be the term given to the exercise of identifying the hazards and calculating the risks.
■ 'Risk control' should be the term given to taking action to eliminate the risk.

SOME GENERAL CONSIDERATIONS

- LEA guidance followed
- levels of responsibility according to age of pupils

Special Needs/Medical Considerations/Age/Group Issues:
- individual needs addressed
- knowledge of medical background
- extra supervision required?
- expertise of extra adult help
- implications for following aspects below

Changing Procedures:
- space available
- procedures understood
- showering facility
- slippery wet floor
- jewellery
- hair tied back/loose beaded hair
- clothing appropriate to the activity

Movement to Working Areas:
- procedures for moving to the area
- hazards on the way
- orderly
- adequate supervision and control
- appropriate behaviour
- safe carrying of equipment
- transport – safe embarkation/disembarkation?
    - seatbelts used
    - driver requirements/responsibilities
    - no distractions

Fire Regulations:
- escape routes clear
- mat storage
- extinguishers present and maintained
- training needed?
- effective emergency communication

First Aid Arrangements:
- responsible person
- training
- first aid kits
- post-accident procedures

Working Areas:
- hazard free – sharp corners, piano, chairs etc.
- sufficient space
- safe surface – grit, glass, splinters, slippery, holes, leaves, ice, water etc.
- dog/horse faeces

Lesson Organisation:
- safe exercise principles – no bouncy stretches/no neck or back over-extension/warm-up and cool-down
- suitability of activity for age/experience
- progression in activities
- recognised and approved practice
- use of available space
- group organisation

Equipment:
- use equipment for purpose it was designed
- suitability of equipment for activity
- maintenance of equipment
- accessibility/storage
- handling, carrying, siting
- check before pupils use it
- sufficient space
- routines for collection, retrieval, changing
- procedures for use of equipment

Staffing:
- confidence and expertise
- necessary qualifications
- non-teacher support/supervision – e.g. parents, coaches, NNEBs, ancillary helpers, students, older pupils
- ratios

Emergency Action:
- contact with school/emergency services if off-site
- contingency plan needed?
- supervision of main group and injured party
- post-accident procedures
- evaluation

FIG 3.1
The risk assessement form: Aspects to consider

Risk assessment

European Standards, progressively replacing British Standards, advocate three levels of risk assessment:

1. A *daily assessment* which is a visual check for obvious hazards. The class teacher would do this at the beginning of each lesson, involving the children in a manner appropriate to their age. This assessment would not be recorded unless some defect was noticed and reported. This is the regular safety check teachers have carried out for many years.

2. *A quarterly (or termly) assessment* which is a visual and/or tactile check on the operation and stability of any equipment and working surface and a brief review of existing procedures relating to the subject area, or facility. This could be carried out by the subject coordinator. A record should be kept of this, simply being re-signed and dated each term unless further action becomes necessary. The record could be that from the annual assessment; a second record is unnecessary.

3. *An annual assessment* which would check the mechanical aspects, of any large and specialist equipment, by a specialist company, and all aspects of the site. A written report would evolve from this. In addition, the staff should collectively review the routine procedures, activities and facilities to ensure that a common and safe system continues to be in place. This should be recorded in a similar way to the termly assessment.

Failure to ensure risk management is carried out, with any necessary action taken, may result in the Health and Safety Executive issuing improvement or prohibition orders or, as a last resort, seeking the imposition of fines or imprisonment through the courts. For example, the proprietor of a play centre for pre-school children failed to comply with improvement notices issued by the local council under Section 4 of the Health and Safety Act. A gas cylinder was not stored safely and a rope bridge had deteriorated constituting a danger to those using it. The court upheld the conviction for the failure to take remedial action (*Moualem v. CCC, 1995*). In another instance the National Association for Head Teachers provided guidance to its members following the imposition of a £21,000 fine by the Health and Safety Executive, equating to a teacher's salary for the extra supervision deemed to be necessary, when a boy drowned during a swimming lesson.

The process of risk management is straightforward and based on common sense but does cause teachers concern. This may be due to what they feel to be threatening terminology. If so, they should think of it as a safety check. It may also be due to the requirement to keep a written record – something not required before 1994. The record is not binding. Rather, it is like the MOT certificate for a car: it shows that at the particular time of the record being made reasonable forethought had been given to what may cause harm. If the circumstances change, then a new assessment and record is made. The exercise is most effectively carried out as a staff group so that all ideas and views are considered and all, through the exercise, are made aware of the necessary procedures. Very little time is needed and part of a series of staff meetings could be used to assess the risks relating to the buildings generally, science, art, design and technology, physical education, off-site activities and any other aspect deemed necessary.

A lack of understanding of the formal terminology and of the process itself may also cause concern. A *hazard* is something with the potential to cause harm. The first stage of the risk management process is to identify any hazards that may cause harm. This is best achieved by thinking through the activity or procedure to identify when, how and where injury may be caused – such as congested areas, poor lighting, slippery floors, projections, unguarded kilns, particular spillages, substances, sharp equipment, certain activities or lack of staff expertise. It is helpful to think logically through the lesson, activity or procedure to identify what may happen in each phase. For example, in a gymnastics lesson, is there anything in the accommodation, equipment, procedures or activities which may cause harm:

- when the children collect their physical education bags, e.g. low hooks or coats left on the floor?
- when they are changing?
- as they move to the hall, e.g. stairs?
- during the warm up, floor work and apparatus sections of the lesson, e.g. a wet patch on the hall floor?
- as they return to the classroom?
- when they change again?
- when they replace their kit?

The second stage of the process is to then evaluate the level of risk by considering how severe any injury arising from the hazard is likely to be and how likely the hazard is to cause injury. Some sources advocate a mathematical calculation multiplying severity on a scale of 1–5 (very minor to serious/fatal) with likelihood, also on a scale of 1–5 (improbable to almost certain). In practice an overall professional judgment fulfils this. By considering the hazard, such as a prominent, sharp projection in a hall, where a fast moving physical education lesson is to take place, a teacher can evaluate the significance of the risk. First by mentally evaluating severity and likelihood, then by judging how frequently and how severe an injury would be incurred, a teacher can determine whether some remedial action is

FIG 3.2
Calculating risk

RISK RATING			
	Likelihood and severity	**Example**	**Action required**
INSIGNIFICANT	■ improbable minor injury such as abrasions	■ supervising children onto a coach in the playground	■ maintain supervision and current practice
MODERATE	■ minor injury possible	■ supervising children onto a coach outside the school gates via a narrow gateway	■ report the situation and discuss whether further action is necessary
SIGNIFICANT	■ probable serious injury such as fractures, eye-loss, paralysis or death	■ inadequate supervision of children onto a coach where they have to cross a busy main road	■ immediate action needed to eliminate the risk – probably by repair, replacement, modification or discontinuing use

necessary for the safety of the children. Teachers need to trust such professional judgments and respond accordingly because calculating risk is essentially informed common sense. A judgment of insignificant, moderate or severe risk, as set out in Figure 3.2, could suffice. Such a model is also used by The National Playing Fields Association.

Identification of hazards and level of risk may be helped by reviewing the school's accident record forms. Further statistical data from agencies such as the Royal Society for the Prevention of Accidents (RoSPA), the National Playing Fields Association (NPFA) or CLEAPS, professional association reviews of national or local guidelines, litigation, and staff discussion of 'near misses' can also be used to identify hazards. Such sources will identify issues requiring further consideration, which may be beyond the experience of the staff.

Current practice is taken into account when determining the level of risk. While a significant hazard may be identified, the existing procedures may adequately control the risk giving a subsequent lower risk rating. It is important that such procedures are documented, that all staff are apprised of these and that they put them into practice consistently, otherwise the risk rating should not be lowered. In many instances existing practice is sufficient to eliminate or minimise the risk. If so, current practice can be continued.

Rating risk in this way is simple, easy to judge and enables informed decisions to be made by weighting the urgency for action to be taken. Only significant risks need immediate action. Moderate risks should be considered but maintaining a watchful eye on these may be sufficient.

Risk assessments must be recorded where there are five or more employees. Pupils are not employees, they are visitors. Virtually every school will need to record assessments because the LEA will be the employer for most very small schools. Grant maintained and private schools are likely to have more than five employees. Even without it being a requirement, the recording of formal risk assessments is good practice in risk management. There are several risk assessment models in circulation (Griffin, 1996, Appendix 3.1; Jones and Lane, 1997; *Together Safely* RoSPA, 1996; CAPT, 1996). Most LEAs offer guidance on risk assessment and schools would be wise to consider available materials. The MHSWR, 1992, stipulates that risk assessment records must indicate:

■ the significant hazards, e.g. the use of some chemicals in science lessons
■ any further action needed, e.g. pupils and staff to wear goggles during some practical work
■ who might be affected, i.e. commonly the pupils and, possibly, the staff
■ that the risk assessment has been carried out, i.e. by completing a form or by displaying an appropriate warning.

No further guidance is given within the 1992 regulations. How the risk assessment was carried out need not be shown. This allows freedom in how the record is expressed but consideration may also need to be given to the form being (for example)

■ user friendly, in format and explanation
■ simple, easily understood
■ efficient and easily completed
■ sufficient to record all that is necessary.

Examples of record formats can be found in *School Health and Safety Management* (Croner, 1995), Physical Education for Key Stages 1 and 2 (BAALPE, 1995), see Figure 3.3, or *Managing Risk Assessment* (NAHT, PM008, 1996). If the risk assessment has been made for a specific event, such as a day excursion to an open air museum, it is good practice after the event to review the record and note any particular hazard, risk or action which should be included in the risk assessment next time. Keep all risk assessment records for future reference. This will save time and effort for visits, journeys and events that are repeated.

School: _____   Work area: _____

ASPECTS TO CONSIDER (list only actual hazards)	SATISFACTORY? (tick ✓)		WHO IS AFFECTED?	IS FURTHER ACTION NECESSARY – RISK CONTROL (Comment)		
	YES	NO	Staff (S) Pupils (P) Visitors (V)	What	By When	Completed?
Special Needs/Medical Considerations/Age/Group Issues						
Changing Procedures						
Movement to Working Areas (including transport)						
Work Area						
Fire Regulations						

FIG 3.3
Risk assessment for physical education

School: .... Work area: ....

ASPECTS TO CONSIDER (list only actual hazards)	SATISFACTORY? (tick ✓)		WHO IS AFFECTED?	IS FURTHER ACTION NECESSARY – RISK CONTROL (Comment)		
	YES	NO	Staff (S) Pupils (P) Visitors (V)	What	By When	Completed?
First Aid Arrangements						
Lesson Organisation/Activity:						
Equipment:						
Staffing:						
Emergency Action:						

Signed: Head teacher ....

Coordinator/Head of Dept: ....

Review 2 .... (Date and initial)

Review 4 .... (Date and initial)

Date of Assessment ....

Review 1 .... (Date and initial)

Review 3 .... (Date and initial)

Review 5 .... (Date and initial)

FIG 3.3
Cont'd

Risk control

If any significant risk is identified, which current practice does not eliminate or minimise, then that risk must be controlled by taking some sort of action. The action may involve:
- removing the risk completely
- trying a less risky option
- preventing access to the hazard
- re-organising the group, activity or procedure to reduce the likelihood of the hazard causing harm
- providing or requiring protective equipment to be used
- improving the staff ratios or providing more information, tuition or training.

It is only when further action such as this needs to be taken that detail needs to be set out on the risk assessment record. The necessary action should then be implemented and consistently applied.

Review of records

Risk assessment records for physical education, science, art, design technology and other areas should be reviewed periodically. Review should occur annually or when circumstances change such as different pupils, different staff, different facilities, different activities or changes due to building work and other such circumstances. In practice the record may simply be re-dated to show that a new risk assessment has been carried out but no change in practice is necessary.

The MHSWR also requires that employees, i.e. teachers, be informed about risks identified by the assessment and any preventative action to be put into practice. In schools, teachers would then be required to implement these for the safety of the pupils, themselves and anyone else affected by the risk. Again, this is simply common sense to ensure consistent safe practice but effective communication of any changes is essential. For example, if the use of an item of equipment was modified in design and technology, then all staff, and subsequently all pupils, would need to be effectively informed. The regulations also require risk management to be carried out by a competent person. This means someone with the knowledge and expertise to foresee possible hazards and risk in their area of work. This is usually the curriculum coordinator for a subject area but the head teacher and governors retain ultimate responsibility because they manage the site and therefore manage the risk. It is important that the competent person receives any training, information and support deemed to be necessary. Sufficient time to fulfil the function is also necessary.

A member of the senior management team usually coordinates the whole risk management programme across the curriculum, ensuring that the various assessments are performed, recorded, any required action is carried out appropriately, communicated effectively and reviewed at least annually. Managing risk, by assessment and control measures, is a part of a teacher's daily routine. It is good practice to involve pupils, of all ages, in the process, in a manner appropriate to their age or ability, as part of the process of teaching safely and teaching safety (see also CAPT, 1998 and Jones and Lane, 1997). In practice, risk management is simply part of the planning, preparation and presentation good teachers have carried out for years. All in the profession need to exhibit similar thorough forethought. This is readily achieved, for example, using posters on the safe carrying and use of equipment; by asking the pupils to look around the work area at the beginning of a lesson to comment on whether there is anything unsafe and to regularly ask questions on safe practice during lessons.

A continuing lack of understanding results in there being some continued reluctance and, indeed, some ignorance, by teachers about risk management requirements under the 1992 regulations. Risk assessment is not a threat. It is simply good practice and good practice is safe practice.

References

BAALPE (The British Association of Advisers and Lecturers in Physical Education) (1995) *Safe Practice in Physical Education*, Dudley: Dudley LEA.

CAPT (1996) *The Risk Pack–A Teacher's Resource*.

CAPT (1998) *Lessons for Safety: Teacher's Guide for Key Stages 1 and 2*, Child Safety Resource Pack.

GRIFFIN, M. (1996) 'Risk assessment for pupils and schools', *The Head's Legal Guide Bulletin*, **29**, July.

JONES, L. and LANE, M. (1997) *Together Safely*, Safer Pupils Resource Pack, London: University of Greenwich.

OFSTED (1998) *Secondary Education 1993–7, A Review of Secondary Schools in England*, London: The Stationery Office.

NAHT (1996) *Managing Risk Assessment*, pp. 6–7, West Sussex: National Association of Head Teachers.

RoSPA (1996) *Together Safely – Policy into Practice*, Birmingham: Royal Society for the Prevention of Accidents.

Legal case studies

Donoghue v. Stevenson, 1932, AC 562 (HL)

Williams v. Eady, 1893, 10 TLR 41 (CA)

Lyes v. Middlesex County Council, 1962, 61 LGR, 443

Wilsher v. Essex Health Authority, 1986, 3AU ER801 (CA)

Qualcast Ltd v. Jaynes, 1959, 2 AU ER 38

Bolton v. Stone, 1951, AC 850

Jeffrey v. London County Council, 1954, 52 LGR 521

Van Oppen v. Clerk to the Bedford Charity Trustees, 1989

Moualem v. Carlisle City Council, 1995, ELR 22

Appendix 3.1 Risk assessment: An example of good practice

Griffin, M. (1996, p. 6) *A Risk Assessment Model*

Is there a danger?
(Hazard recognition)

How likely is it to happen?
(Risk identification)

How serious would it be?
(Possible outcomes)

Can anything be done to reduce the likelihood or severity?
(Options for control)

How is the order of priority for controls decided?
(Priorities)

What is going to be done and by whom?
(Record/plan action)

Is the risk now acceptable?
Will it continue so to be?
(Evaluation, monitoring and review)

Does the process work for different activities?
(Transferability)

Part two

Chapter 4

Safety in design and technology
John Twyford

Design and Technology (D&T) education awakens and stimulates children's capabilities to design and make things for given, or found, purposes. Pupils' learning is centred on the human ability to design products that look good, as well as to make things that work well for specified purposes. It is in these contexts that pupils can demonstrate their creativity and technical skill to innovate and modify products and systems in the light of the National Curriculum.

Children's D&T capabilities are also developed through their direct practical experience of the typical everyday things, tools and machines, that people use and own. In so many ways, pupils acquire knowledge and skills concerning how things are used and work, or are maintained and treasured. Experience of these basic human skills and feelings involve knowing how to hold, fashion, cut, stick, or fit together components, how things might break, scratch, slide, roll, turn, pour and fall over or stand up – especially those products that pupils create themselves. It naturally follows that being safe in their work, as well as respectful of health issues concerning how things are used, are also dynamic factors in children's success in D&T education.

The National Curriculum in D&T requires pupils to learn from a range of assignments, tasks and activities, especially those that provide opportunities for them to put their personal ideas to a test. An awareness of how and why people use things, including the different values they place upon them is all part of the spectrum of capabilities required under the statutory Orders. Thus, the formal curriculum focuses upon how children acquire certain design skills and technical competence in making things. This curriculum explicitly requires children gain knowledge and understanding in health and safety for example, at KS1:

> ❛ . . . *simple knowledge and understanding of health and safety, as consumers and when working with materials and components, including: considering the hazards and risks in their activities; following simple instructions to control risk to themselves . . .*

and also at KS2:

> ❛ . . . *recognise hazards to themselves and to others in a range of products, activities and environments; assessing risks to themselves and to others; taking action to control these risks . . .* (DfE, D&T NC, 1995, pp. 3 and 5)

In providing these experiences, it is the task of teachers to reveal, and make clear, the knowledge, skills, understanding and values that comprise D&T capabilities. The actual subject matter should be wide ranging because issues and contexts, not merely procedures, skills or facts alone, determine D&T. A key way for D&T education to fulfil these overarching learning purposes is for children and teachers to work safely. The well-being of both pupils and teachers is derived from the safe, confidence to tackle this exciting subject.

It follows that safe and healthy practices in designing and making things should be based upon controlled, disciplined and systematic approaches to teaching and learning in D&T study. Therefore, H&S (Health and Safety) should be broadly reinforced and integrated within pupils' work and expectations, as study progresses from one scheme to another. This approach will enable pupils to fully grasp the value and significance of H&S issues. Merely delivering safety issues exclusively through separate sessions, or presenting it at the beginning of each practical assignment, task or activity – just for safety's sake – should not be the mainstay of its presentation to children. Holistic approaches to creative designing and making are the essential characteristics of the function of D&T education.

Teaching health and safety in D&T

Teachers are not qualified to teach unless they clearly demonstrate appropriate knowledge and understanding of H&S issues within their specialist subject. Importantly, the Standards for the Award of Qualified Teacher Status (QTS) (DfEE Circular 4/98) states that for student teachers to acquire knowledge and understanding in their D&T work within a Primary course:

Those to be awarded QTS must, when assessed, demonstrate that . . . (d) for each core and specialist subject covered in their training . . . (viii) [they] are familiar with subject-specific health and training requirements, where relevant, and plan lessons to avoid potential hazards. (DfEE, 1998, p. 10)

In support of these professional requirements, The Design and Technology Association, (DATA) proposed draft guidelines for *Standards for Safety Training in D&T*, which were put together by a wide group of subject specialists. The work was commissioned by the Teacher Training Agency (TTA) and after due consideration of details and consultation, it is likely they will become a H&S requirement in both primary and secondary schools. As envisaged by DATA, the provision of H&S is promoted as vital to the growth of good practice and performance for both teachers and children. It is an essential component of a teacher's qualification, especially in D&T education. The introductory statement concerning primary D&T states, that:

 . . . when planning and conducting design and technology activities students and teachers must give due regard to the health and safety of themselves and their pupils. They must be aware of current relevant health and safety responsibilities, legislation and liability. (DATA, 1997b, p. 10)

These are the broad responsibilities that underpin the teacher's duty of care. DATA also offers guidance on standards in safety in primary education. This is structured in such a way as to represent the essential issues concerning the provision of H&S in D&T education, see Figure 4.1. The concept of minimum standards in H&S is to be applauded since they clearly define teachers' responsibilities in fulfilling their duty of care in D&T. Knowing

FIG 4.1
Essential issues concerning the provision of Health and Safety in D&T education

Overall standards for class teachers: These are the minimum standards for all class teachers teaching design and technology. Students and teachers must demonstrate both personal and professional competence in that they:

- are able to undertake risk assessment to highlight potential dangers and hazards
- know that they should regularly ensure that the environment is not a health and safety hazard and be able to organise working spaces to minimise risks
- have secure knowledge and understanding of tools, processes and equipment before they use them themselves and with their pupils
- know and be able to apply appropriate regulations for the materials and components they use, taking account of storage, fumes, dust, microbiological hazard, skin contact and other allergic reactions and interactions
- adopt appropriate teaching strategies, understanding the common misconceptions, mistakes, possible risks and pupil management issues associated with design and technology activities.

(DATA, 1997, p. 10)

about H&S and how to enable children to work safely, as well as in a healthy environment, are vital professional skills, now formally required as part of teachers' qualifications and professional responsibilities.

Throughout, it is important that broadly agreed standards and procedures are supported and embraced because then all teachers and student teachers will be made aware of how to deal with H&S, as part of their job specification and professional responsibilities. The notion of national standards should also be supported, as it provides a framework for 'regular and approved' practice. This is because safety should not be left to individual experience but featured as a clear component of good practice in teaching. Working safely is an indicator of sound knowledge and skills in designing and making in all classrooms.

Safe and healthy D&T practice in the classroom

Essentially, children acquire safe practices over time. In the author's experience throughout all phases of children's education in D&T, pupils are aided in this through being exposed to good practice based on correct procedure. This includes clear and consistent expectations that certain things are done in particular ways, because they are recognised as correct and effective techniques in skilful work. Sharp tools handled properly are better than blunt tools. Calm attitudes, and well-motivated approaches to the work at hand, support effective safe practice in D&T work. Thus, acquiring safe practice is vital to success.

Teachers have the well-being of their students at heart and they are prepared to create healthy, safe working environments for all concerned. However, at times, some teachers lack confidence in their own technical understanding of D&T practice. This tends to prevent them from enabling children to gain the full value of D&T study. In this regard, it is the aim of the minimum standards in H&S to overcome such concerns. But it must be recognised that 'legislation' and 'requirements' alone do not ensure safe practice. Implementation is essential. For example, a teacher not knowing that a fuse had 'gone' in a hot glue gun thought that the glue gun was broken and unusable. This prevented a range of pupils' work from being completed. The teacher was frightened of the glue gun and what it does, and did not really want to use it. Once it appeared not to work it was abandoned. But, simply switching off the power and unplugging the gun, then unscrewing the plug to change the fuse – a safety feature – and replacing the correct fuse is a common and necessary task. Also, placing a working glue gun in a safe area to work, at a useful working height for children, away from crowded classroom situations, and with the flex free to move when used, including using a stand for the gun to rest on when not being used, makes the glue gun's use effective and within the basic control of both teachers and children. Knowing what to do if hot glue gets onto skin is also important. Running cold water on the burn is the first aid. My experience in schools suggests this rarely happens.

Above all, knowing how to use any tool effectively should provide the teacher with the necessary confidence to take appropriate action to enable children to make successful products. A tool, like a glue gun, should be used because it will enable children to understand a specific way to join materials, cleanly and with skill. It should not be used to hold components together because more appropriate ways of joining would take too long to do or require more expensive materials. When teachers know the purpose of tools, including how best they can be used, then D&T work will flourish. The standards, the NC and professional associations all require teachers to fully understand the operation of such tools. These new guidelines and standards should help alleviate any lack of confidence and technical understanding.

Naturally, throughout children's D&T work, issues of safety must be made clear and reinforced. The elements of risk in D&T need to be managed and, as much as possible, foreseen. A certain formality is required in teaching and demonstrating procedures and techniques. Overall, safety issues should enhance the pleasure of practical work. As over caution can at times remove the challenge and thrill from some work, it is important that safety issues should complement the work rather than put limits upon it. Further, if the teacher ends up doing all the 'tricky bits' all of the time, then the validity of the work should be questioned. There are times when a little help from adults enables children to be safe and successful. But, for the most part, children should do their own designing and making, especially within the gambit of the requirements of the teaching of D&T capabilities in the National Curriculum.

Importantly, at KS2, pupils are to be taught the:
- knowledge and understanding of health and safety as designers, makers and consumers, including recognising hazards to themselves and to others in a range of products, activities and environments
- assessing risks to themselves and to others
- taking action to control these risks (DfEE D&T NC, 1995, p. 5)

Teachers are therefore charged not only to teach safely but to teach safety. As teachers take on board the spirit of designing and making to provide their pupils with an effective D&T education, their professional training and development should equip them with the skills to educate pupils in H&S. Teachers should brief themselves thoroughly on the DATA standards as these are a clear indication of the latest requirements. Further, head teachers are given legal guidelines for D&T work. For example,

> *The arrangements of furniture, use of effective general lighting and the wiring regulations of the Institute of Electrical Engineers, should be followed . . . In the interests of safety, workshops should be warm (cold hands are less sensitive than warm ones), clean and as clear of clutter as possible . . . rooms should be swept up regularly . . . Safety signs and colours should be used to warn of dangers and clearly worded precautionary notices should be prominently displayed.*
> (Croner, The Head's Legal Guide, 1986, p. 141)

Professionally, there is a great deal of guidance available to assist good practice in H&S. Teachers have to make decisions about children's D&T work. For example, when are children expected to work with certain tools? When should they be taught the safe use of things? How do children progress from one level of skill to the next? Increasingly, many of the answers to these questions can be found in regular and approved practice, which features as part of the professional training of teachers. For example, what does the collective professional teaching experience of different people using scissors tell us about when children should use scissors independently? Is there a law of life that says that only at a certain age can people use scissors? Many classroom teachers have their views about when, how and what type of scissors children should use. Will the judgments about scissors enable decisions about knives, needles, saws, and glue guns to be made? Is it reasonable that every tool should have a prescribed age restriction that everyone must adopt? What is really needed is a practical understanding of the safe use of appropriate tools, including an appreciation of the risks, while not allowing them to inhibit achievement of educational goals.

In answer to these questions, the NC requires that children should be shown safe practice, and should also be drawn into the exposition of the skill or process being demonstrated, as much as possible. In this way children can be directly engaged in learning safety rather than merely being told about it. Is it not enough that children are shown the safe use of things. Safety comes with experience of understanding good practice. Collective safety is a responsibility of the teacher, and it is the character of the subject matter being studied, as well as the discipline of classroom management, that are the crucial factors in safe practice in D&T.

Safety is also a responsibility of children, because they are entrusted with certain opportunities in which they should play their part. Responsibility is something that should be given to individuals so that they know what it means to be responsible, rather than being told to be responsible. Being safe and healthy is part of being social and part of a community. Thus, teachers should provide clear messages about a whole range of safety issues, including the part children play in it. Children should not merely learn certain rules. They should in time, and in non-stressful circumstances, be shown and guided in the safe use of things. Teachers are therefore charged to find and facilitate design assignments in which children can build their subject capabilities. Pupils should be enabled to choose artefacts to make, as well as materials and tools, and be taught to handle them safely. In this way they will make good quality products and gain the personal confidence to achieve more complex skills. Therefore, D&T teachers should consider the relationship between children's design ideas and the practical manufacturing required to bring about a successful outcome. Children should make what they have designed, rather than be constrained to design only what they can make, perhaps because using certain tools or materials is problematic. However, in establishing a series of practical assignments, tasks and activities that form appropriate structures and strategies for children's learning, teachers should also test the technical feasibility of each practical task to be undertaken.

D&T essentially offers opportunities for open-ended activities in which it is not always possible to predict what might happen. Because these opportunities allow children to do things that do not have any set answers, there may be a certain amount of tension concerning children's safety. But children need these opportunities to do things that do not have set answers as it is in the nature of both creative and technical design. Good classroom management is vital in this regard, so too is motivating children, through their interests and their developing technical skills to produce authentic, well-made original products.

Minor accidents are common place and need to be dealt with in a common sense way, within recognised classroom practice and first aid regulations. Horrible accidents are fortunately very rare, nevertheless, in the event of an accident teachers should know how to deal with it.

It is sensible that teachers prepare children in the safe use of tools, places to work and the whole working environment. A range of safety codes concerning tools – scissors, scalpels, saws and especially holding devices, for example, a vice, glues, ways of testing things, food hygiene, heating things and using electricity – are generally prescribed within the ambit of school working conditions. Special reference should be made to preparing materials, cutting, shaping, drilling, joining and holding safely a range of typical materials in the case studies offered in this work.

Experience also informs us that there is little need to be alarmist about doing D&T in classrooms. A very useful approach to managing D&T is to provide an area dedicated to this work. This enables both teachers and pupils to maintain continuity. If things are constantly being stored and put away, got out and put away again, as is so often the case, then these processes tend to create problems. At worst, work can be damaged or lost. Being able to leave work and return to it, and to work in an area that can cope with storing tools and materials, not only gives a clear identity to practical work, but also preserves the work far better.

Children and teachers need to be able to anticipate and to recognise danger. This includes knowing how to read instructions and interpret signs or symbols.

> *Teachers of subjects involving practical work . . . are not only concerned with preventing accidents but also with safety education as an essential part of their work.* (DES, 1981, p. 1)

The philosophy of the Association for Science Education is that:

> *. . . in primary schools science is very much, and should be, an open-ended activity. As such it is not always possible to predict all the problems which might occur. Safety standards should be higher than those found at home. Primary schools are extremely safe places with few reported accidents . . .* (ASE, 1990, p. 4)

This approach is also vital to the success of D&T education. It is recognised by the guidelines given in *Make it Safe*, by the National Association of Advisers and Inspectors in Design and Technology, and DATA's *Managing Resources and Health and Safety* (both very useful well-written books concerning the safe practice in practical work.) They reinforce the notion that:

> *Design and Technology activities in primary schools are, for the most part, safe – and great fun! A few simple precautions will enable teachers to work with confidence and provide a rich experience for children.* (DATA, 1997a, sec. 4)

If teachers adopt this spirit of working, as well as trial and prototype any practical work, then their pupils can gain the full value of success in developing of their D&T capabilities. They can also establish personal confidence to tackle the subject safely, through knowledge and skill.

Safety principles and procedures

The author during recent work in primary schools has tested the following information, procedures and principles. Importantly, they are based on identifying risks and establishing safety procedures – all of which were agreed, discussed and developed with the support of experienced teachers. They offer conclusions about what children will do as a class or as groups of individuals, minimising risks within the working environment and the D&T work itself and guidance on planning safe work in D&T in the primary classroom.

Consideration of the RISKS involved in teaching groups of children D&T so that:
- The work is compatible with what can reasonably be expected of children
- The assignments, tasks or activities are reviewed for the risks inherent in their manufacture and subsequent use
- The maturity and background experience of students is understood and considered
- The children are familiar with their working environment and ways of being in the room
- The tools and machines required are understood in the context of their use
- The pupils are not engaged in moving machinery or equipment unnecessarily or beyond their capabilities
- The pupils use non-hazardous materials
- The skills required to use the tools are taught and not assumed
- The use of special clothing, including tying back hair where necessary, is appropriately instituted.

In minimising RISKS through room management strategies involving the use of tools and materials, teachers should:
- Consider risks in classroom layout, so that classroom management strategies cover safe seating and movement in the room, especially when children are required to obtain materials and tools
- Provide instruction in the use of scissors and other hand tools to be followed by light supervision, with particular care in relation to movement in the room
- Demonstrate the use of craft knives, including the importance of using cutting mats, metal rulers, and the skill of working away from the hand and the body
- Discuss the selection and use of appropriate adhesives
- Observe children working in pairs or at a specified pace, allowing children to move to collect tools or materials under instruction
- Provide specified areas for cutting operations
- Encourage children in good D&T practices, through neat and effective working habits, as well as to enable children to plan their manufacturing activities by using their designs
- Know the boundaries for testing products, e.g. firing a projectile, flying kites or testing a pull-along toy.

FIG 4.2
A ballistic device which
uses leverage and not an
elastic band

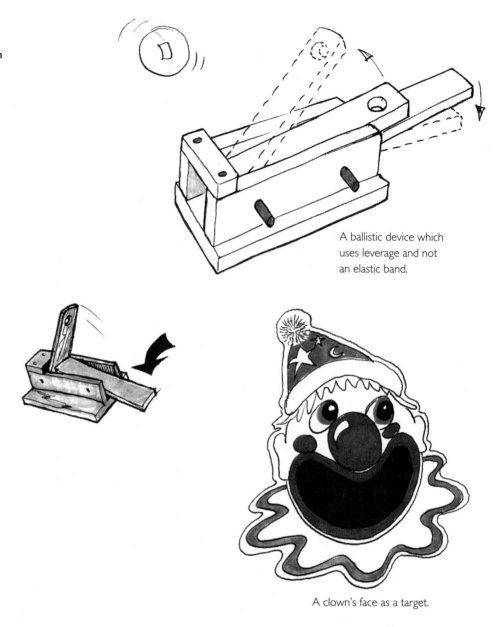

A ballistic device which
uses leverage and not
an elastic band.

A clown's face as a target.

These broad issues are used to establish and demonstrate safe working for a typical scheme of work in D&T. Making a ballista to fire a ping pong ball is given here as an example (see Figure 4.2).

As noted, the formal curriculum requires health and safety issues to be addressed within D&T assignments, tasks or activities. In the 'ballista' task, as illustrated in a student teachers' design sheet (Figure 4.3), pupils should be aware that in designing the product, and solving the problem of projecting

BALLISTICS

AIM :- To design and make a device which will fire five pieces of ammunition e.g. a ping-pong ball, three metres into a target, in this case a clown's mouth.

DESIGN PROCESS :- I started off by sketching a few ideas. I knew there were limits on the designs – no machine saws could be used or saws so only traditional methods could be employed to make the model. We were shown books on Roman designs for ballistas – ancient military engines for hurling stones, which I took as a starting point but soon decided the simpler the design probably the better. My first idea was to have just one support post for the model but it became evident that this may not have enough support when the model was fired, (near right.) so I decided on two support posts to give the structure strength, (far right.)

THE PROCESS :-

Craft techniques such as using dowel rod to join components was introduced in this project because of the limited availability of certain tools in the Primary school. Having selected a base I attached two support posts using the dowel rods. A piece of dowel was placed through the support posts to hold the firing device which held a "carrier" to hold the ping-pong balls. I decided the top half of the firing device should be longer than the bottom half to give a greater trajectory. When the device was released. A rubber band was linked through the bottom of the firing device and stretched around the base to increase tension. All holes were drilled using 6mm screw and 6mm dowel rods, used to join components. (see diagram right.)

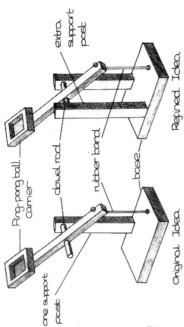

Ping-pong ball carrier

extra support post

dowel rod

rubber band

one support post

base

Original Idea   Refined Idea

The diagram on the left shows the line of flight of the ping-pong ball. The longer top half of the firing device should give it a greater trajectory – the curve of a projectile in its flight through space.

Line of flight

Aim to fire ping-pong ball into clown's mouth.

3 metres away

target

longer top should give greater trajectory

rubber band stocks as device is released.

THE RESULTS :- Although my device had the strength to fire the whole 3 metres (especially once I'd tightened the elastic band), the aim was poor as the arm holding the carrier tended to wobble around a bit. Maybe by putting a bar across the top of the two support posts would give the model more stability and therefore a more accurate aim.

The finished product.

FIG 4.3
A student's design folder on ballistics

a ping pong ball three metres onto a target, they should devise the mechanism to be powerful enough to do its job. In making the product, pupils need to know how to use a range of hand tools safely. Specifically they need to know how to cut to length with a saw, shape materials and join components. The product also has to be safe to use for its design purpose. The ballista should be used appropriately and directed at the target and not used in any other capacity. This component assembly assignment is devised to help children to learn about and use craft skills, to acquire knowledge of choosing materials and handling tools. It is also designed to enable pupils to create a machine that will function for a specified purpose. The task may seem to have a high level of risk but, handled appropriately, it is a good example of purposeful, safe D&T. Also, the issues to be covered in the curriculum are directly used in this work concerning structures and mechanisms.

Short focused practical tasks to enable children to use materials and tools correctly should be devised to support these creative assignments. Risk assessment by the children can form part of these tasks. Also, design evaluation activities, which enable pupils to see how things work, can be used to indicate how products operate safely or otherwise. Children should be shown how certain products have built-in safety features. For example, an electric kettle made from an insulating material prevents the user being burnt if it is touched, other than on its handle. This understanding can be used to inculcate not only design appreciation, but also understanding of potential hazards in the product itself and how it might be used or misused. Thus, both teachers and children should know how to form a risk assessment in their D&T work. They should actively use the nature of the subject to work safely, and to see how everyday artefacts are subjected to tests and scrutiny concerning their safe handling, storage and maintenance.

Practical task – modelling a siege machine

This project requires pupils to make a functional product based on their problem-solving and decision-making abilities. Children should design a 'siege machine' so that both the ballistic mechanism and the structure enable a missile to be fired straight at a target (see Figure 4.2). The work involves assembling components in resistant materials, as well as the idea of devising a constructional kit. The project is a useful vehicle for introducing craft techniques, for example, using dowel rods to join components.

The pupils' design brief is to design and make a device that will fire five ping pong balls, three metres into a target, for example a clown's mouth.

FIG 4.4
Basic craft techniques
required in making a
ballistic device

Using a try square

Drilling holes safely using a
hand drill and vice

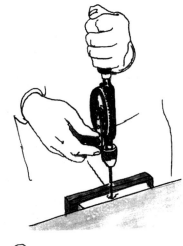

Sawing to length using a hand saw and bench
hook securely clamped to a bench in a vice

Using a dowel rod to join materials
or create swivelling mechanism

They will need to learn the following techniques and use the outlined
materials. The project involves knowing how to

■ measure lengths (although some might be guessed at), squareness, the use
of a try square, cutting wood to length using a hand saw, a bench hook, a
vice and a woodwork bench
■ shape wood with rasps and files, as well as with glass paper; and join
components with the aid of dowels; use a 6.0 mm drill bit for tight joints
and 6.5 mm drill bit for moving joints or swivelling parts; drill using a
hand drill into a scrap of wood or with the material held in a vice;
hammer in the dowel rods when required.

Some of these basic techniques used in making a ballistic device are
illustrated in Figure 4.4. Pupils should also have access to and choose from a
variety of resistant materials.

FIG 4.5
Three solutions to
ballistic mechanisms –
Children's examples

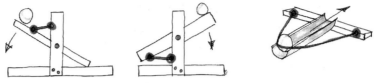

Three solutions to ballistic mechanisms

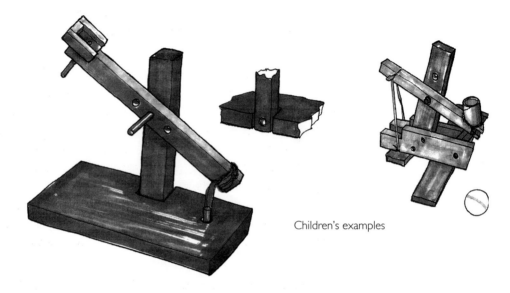

Children's examples

This case study is typical of a D&T assignment, ideal for juniors and is compatible with what can reasonably be expected of children working in this context. Figure 4.5 illustrates examples of pupils own ballistic mechanisms. Pupils should have some craft experience and knowledge of workshop practice in a classroom familiar to them. If they have little or no craft experience, then this project is an ideal starting point for using 'resistant materials' to create a working mechanism.

It is advisable for teachers to work through the project themselves to establish the pace and skill of the work, as well as to ensure that there are sufficient tools and materials for children to successfully achieve a working ballista. In this way, the safety issues will become apparent; if they do not, then it is useful to seek advice concerning the feasibility of a project of this nature.

Many teachers have large class groups. This will require the teacher to use different forms of organisation; for example, to stagger the work for pupils. Certainly pupils can work on their designs while their classmates make their machine and visa versa. In this project the room should be organised to accommodate workbenches with vices, bench hooks and effective ways of clamping down work – a vital safety procedure! Children will be required:

- to cut wood to length with junior hacksaws, hand saws and coping saws;
- to shape the wood; and
- to drill two specified size holes (deliberately chosen to minimise problems): one for joining, (6 mm), rather like using nails (do not use nails at all for this project!); the other to provide a swivel point (6.5 mm) for the moving component in the machine.

Wood adhesive can also be used, but is not essential. These are typical practical issues, which the teacher has to manage through a clear plan of action suitable to the working environment. Thus, the classroom layout should enable pupils to remain at a work station rather than move around the room, unless they require materials and tools, in which case they should work to the established routines for these tasks. Hand tools will suffice throughout and pupils should work individually or in pairs. The skills required to use the tools should be rehearsed and demonstrated to pupils. They should be drawn into demonstrations of how to saw, how to drill and how to shape the materials. Children should wear aprons.

Instruction in the use of hand tools should be followed by light supervision, with particular care in relation to movement in the room. Teachers should place themselves in a strategic position in the room from which to observe what all children are doing, all of the time. From such a vantage point the teacher can also encourage pupils in good practice, especially by checking careful and effective working habits.

A siege machine is designed for use. The experiment to see who has made an effective machine should be set up so that pupils can safely test their machines away from the working craft activities. When all the machines are made, pupils should be required to test them individually, from a designated point, three metres from the target, at bench height. Pupils should not fire their machines at will at any point in the lesson. In this way they must learn the boundaries for testing and using the product. This example has been chosen because it requires knowledge about safety issues, about making as well as using a machine in the classroom. Thus, children should not only design and make things, but more importantly know how to use them for the purposes intended. In a disciplined and sound working environment children concentrate well on their assignments. They are usually keen to show how they can 'get things right', and to engage in making things.

> *The most striking attitude expressed by all the children, in an explicit way,*
> *was that they enjoyed their D&T lessons because it involved making things . . .*
> *Similarly, children are able to do this with 'craft-design' processes, especially*
> *the pleasure of the creative processes when manipulating materials . . . Thus,*
> *being directly involved in 'doing' is vital in a sound D&T education, and a*
> *deeply natural thing to do.* (Twyford and Burden, in press, p. 22)

D&T work is seen as a real design challenge to pupils, especially assignments
that require something to be made well.

Acquisition of safe practice in D&T

This section considers safety in D&T assignments, tasks and activities in
relation to subject structure issues, as the teacher's professional judgment
about the curriculum informs safety issues. Formally, safety issues should be
determined from the knowledge and understanding involved in D&T work,
described in the National Curriculum, as well as guidance from OFSTED,
Qualifications, Curriculum and Assessment Authority (QCA), and TTA. The
subject matter in D&T is designed to develop children's capabilities to design
and make with knowledge and understanding. Thus, D&T capabilities
involve three key epistemological issues.

Know-how in designing and making

This represents the acquisition and use of skills, craft techniques, processes,
ways of handling materials and media, as well as the development and
production of products through certain trained capacities to act like
designers or technologists in the classroom. Thus, when pupils experiment
sensitively and creatively with skills, techniques or ideas, they can
experience personal capacity to solve problems and make decisions.

Knowing about ideas and facts through designing and making

This involves disciplined thought about the subject, including common
sense and general knowledge; knowing how to apply information; having a
sense of trends and influences in design; as well as stimulating personal
expression to discover and interpret issues and possibilities for D&T activity.

D&T knowledge is also derived from awareness of precedents, materials,
processes, as well as an understanding of the usefulness of things, including
appreciating how they are evaluated. Establishing D&T issues, clarifying

topics, defining problems, deciding upon solutions and knowing the context for design ideas can be explored by encouraging pupils to reveal what things are for and how to generate ideas. Learning about D&T fosters an understanding of safety issues and knowing how to work safely also encourages pupils' confidence in their D&T studies. A grasp of safety issues helps effective decision-making about materials and methods. During actual production and realisation children learn how to work safely.

The importance of the right attitude

This is concerned with pupils' motivation and attitudes to their work. Knowing how to act safely enables children to form a constructive attitude towards doing D&T. This can be vital in building effective attitudes towards the subject because it requires pupils to play their part in creative thinking and to get things right – safely. Motivation is enhanced by design issues being authentic, although this can be diminished by overbearing approaches to safety.

D&T learning can be rewarding. While there is pleasure in success, the ability to face disappointments also needs to be taken into account. Knowing when to stop working if things are going wrong is very important, because frustration and irritation are the precursors of accidents. With this in mind it is vital that safety enhances pupils' work rather than puts limits upon it. Children work safely when fully engaged in their work. Realistic motivation is the cornerstone of good working practices.

Developing children's understanding of safe practices

In developing children's understanding of health and safety they should discuss and see things being used safely:

Health and Safety is an important part of design and technology. Children should be trained to work safely and sensibly and to understand that their actions can directly affect other children's safety. Children can develop their understanding of health and safety through a range of activities. The teacher can provide opportunities for children to:

- *talk about and write down simple rules for keeping safe during practical work*
- *assess the risks when equipment is placed in an unsafe position*
- *consider the hazards when tools are not correctly used*
- *make safety posters demonstrating safe practice*

■ *talk about reducing risks*

■ *discuss the importance of personal hygiene when preparing for food activities . . .* (DATA, 1997, sec. 4.3.4)

These guidelines have been used successfully by teachers. They also reiterate the fact that safe working comes directly from skilful work and understanding of the subject matter. Teachers should aim to be fully aware of what children can achieve and learn in D&T. This is a task that needs to be addressed constantly and can be assessed by evaluating the different qualities apparent in pupils' work. A firm basis for safe work is the teacher knowing what children actually do and achieve in D&T.

The first hand experiences that D&T education offers children is crucial in giving them a respect for, and confidence in, their own thoughts and skills. It also provides children with a set of workable practices, experiences, tasks and models, why people design and make things. D&T education is also concerned with imparting respect for the capacities of people to innovate and create things. It should leave the student with a sense of the limitlessness of human powers of invention. At its heart is designing and making, and how to bring about change to meet future needs. This goal cannot be fully realised unless all concerned work safely, in healthy environments.

References

ASE (1990) *Be Safe! Some Aspects of Safety in School Science and Technology for Key Stages 1 and 2*, 2nd edn., Hatfield: Association for Science Education.

CRONER (1986) *The Head's Legal Guide*, Loose-leaf document, Kingston-upon-Thames: Croner Publications.

DATA (1997a) *The D&T Primary Coordinators' File*, Wellesbourne: The Design and Technology Association.

DATA (1997b) *Standards for Safety Training in D&T*, draft guidelines, Wellesbourne: The Design and Technology Association.

DES (1981) *Safety in Practical Studies*, London: HMSO.

DFE (1995) *Design and Technology in the National Curriculum*, London: HMSO.

DfEE (1998) *Teaching: High Status, High Standards* (Circular 4/98), London: Department for Education and Employment.

THE NATIONAL ASSOCIATION OF ADVISERS AND INSPECTORS IN DESIGN AND TECHNOLOGY (1992) *Make it Safe.*

TWYFORD, J. and BURDEN, R. (in press) *Primary School Children's Conceptions of Design and Technology as a Curriculum Subject: a Constructivist Approach.*

Chapter 5

Health and safety in the use of ICT in schools

Chris Taylor

The use of computers in education is one area where little consideration has been given to safety issues beyond the obvious matter of electrical safety. Texts produced for teachers about the use of Information and Communication Technologies (ICT) in teaching contain few references, if any, to health and safety aspects of this technology. This chapter seeks to address the issue of safety with regard to ICT more fully and will suggest what best practice might be, given the current state of knowledge and law. It will consider employment law, research into ICT-health related problems, statutory requirements such as those of the National Curriculum and what OFSTED might look for in your school. It then seeks to show how this can be effectively incorporated into classroom and other environments where ICT might be used in a school. It is intended that a teacher might use it in the classroom to plan workstations for the benefit of their pupils. It will also be of use to the ICT coordinator, to help construct policy and inform purchasing plans. It also considers the needs of other employees in education who might have some considerable contact with ICT by virtue of their work.

In terms of safety, a computer system appears ostensibly to pose little risk to the user and its presence in a classroom seems to offer little risk to pupils. Reputable companies produce machines that comply with electrical safety regulations. Except for portables, computers are usually static in use, being placed on a desk or a trolley, and thus may appear to be relatively safe. However, experience of working with ICT has shown me that there are significant safety issues of which every teacher should be aware. These same issues have been used to frame the legal context that surrounds the use of ICT in the workplace via the European Community Directive (EEC) on the use of Visual Display Units (VDUs) (EEC, 1990). The potential hazards are compounded when there are multiple computer systems in one room, for example, in a computer lab. The issues that affect pupils, teachers and other school employees who come into contact with ICT are:

■ Electrical safety
■ Ergonomics (creating a suitable workstation environment)
■ Visual strain and disturbance from VDU use
■ Electro-magnetic radiation
■ Other emissions (dust, noise, etc.).

Employment law and hazards in ICT

Widespread use of VDUs is relatively new, so there has been little time for a case history of safety related matters in employment law to develop. Only over the last 20 years has extended computer use become common place for large numbers of workers. By the time the EEC Directive came into place in 1992, seven million people in Britain were working with VDUs (Nuttall, 1992). There has been a lag in the development of law to deal with problems arising from this. This increasing use has been reflected in schools, with computers being placed in almost every primary school classroom, and computer labs being set up in most secondary schools. In the requirement for Initial Teacher Training, it is expected that 'Trainees must demonstrate that they are aware of the current health and safety legislation relating to the use of computers, and can identify potential hazards and minimise risks.' (TTA, 1998, p. 16) According to the EEC Directive, knowledge of such hazards and their identification is the responsibility of the employer. No information is included in the TTA document, that details the legislation, or identifies the risks, and such information is not readily available! It is certainly not included in any recent texts about ICT in education, or any documents from the DfEE regarding ICT in the National Curriculum.

Pupils in schools do not have the same rights as employees and are not covered by the Factories Acts. However, existing employment law is a good basis from which to start when considering potential risks and how they might be avoided. Teachers, clerical workers and technicians are employees of either LEAs or schools. Those who work with ICT are subject to the requirements of the law and schools should seek to protect them from health risks.

The most important regulation in Britain relating to ICT is the EEC Directive on VDU use (EEC, 1990) which constrains employers to take certain steps to protect employees from harm. This forms a good basis from which to start when considering workstation set up and classroom provision. The main areas considered in this directive cover:

■ Equipment (including the computer keyboard and display screen, work desk and work chair)

■ Working environment with regard to space, lighting, reflections and glare, noise, heat, radiation and humidity

■ Operator/computer interface, in that the computer software should be suited for the task in hand, easy to use and appropriate to the user's experience.

The directive requires that an analysis of all work stations is undertaken by employers 'In order to evaluate the safety and health conditions to which they give rise for their workers, particularly as regards possible risks to eyesight, physical problems and problems of mental stress.' (EEC, 1990, p. 15) Few schools have undertaken such an analysis to the placing of computers in classrooms. Any employee using a computer system for more than an hour a day should be considered to be a significant user. In schools, few children come near to this level of usage for regular periods, although some might come near to it when completing work for assessment. However, many pupils also have computers at home, and the total potential daily usage should be considered when calculating risk. It is also reasonable to assume that children are more vulnerable than adults and require less exposure to cause problems. We do not know how sustained computer use might affect them, but have a duty of care to ensure they are protected from problems which have developed in places of work. The purpose of the legislation is to minimise the risk of the following health problems:

■ The development of Repetitive Strain Injury symptoms due to prolonged keyboard use

■ Postural problems due to prolonged work at inadequate workstations (particularly spinal and neck problems)

■ Visual difficulties caused by sustained concentration on a VDU screen

■ Increased stress and anxiety levels.

Hazards associated with computers

There is now a fair amount of evidence that sustained computer use can cause or make worse a range of physical problems (Wilkins, 1990; Nuttall, 1992). These problems include postural and spinal problems, Repetitive Strain Injury (RSI), and deterioration of eyesight. RSI has been acknowledged as an industrial illness since 1948 and successful cases involving computer use have been brought by employees against their employers, including BT and the *Financial Times* (Nuttall, 1992). Recent research at the University College London, clearly shows that RSI sufferers have serious nerve damage and that this is work related, caused by both keyboard and mouse use (AUT, 1998). Research by Wilkins has shown that flicker from lighting or computer screens can cause headaches and speed up the heart rate. In addition to this, computers contribute to the general deterioration of the workplace environment by means of ionising, heating and drying the atmosphere, creating and adding to the ambient noise levels. There is also evidence that computers and similar machinery (photocopiers, laser printers, fax machines) can contribute to the level of volatile organic compounds in the atmosphere which react with ozone to produce symptoms which fall within the 'sick building syndrome' (Baker, 1997). These might even be poisoning us, with suggestions that such problems could be causing 5,000 cases of cancer per year in the USA (Miller, 1998). The difficulty with this is that this area requires a degree of knowledge and expertise beyond the range of the classroom teacher. With regard to the workplace, it is the duty of the employer to 'Perform an analysis of workstations in order to evaluate the safety and health conditions' and to 'Take appropriate measures to remedy the risks found' (EEC, 1990, p. 15).

There have been other problems associated with VDU use, such as spontaneous abortion of foetuses among pregnant mothers, headaches and general sickness. These have been linked to electro-magnetic emissions from VDUs, although research data to support this is inconclusive. 'The NRPB do not consider that the emissions from a VDU will put either you or your unborn child at risk' (HSE, 1986, p. 1). On the other hand, Bentham (1991) refers to research that indicates exactly the opposite! She quotes research in the USSR and Czechoslovakia that found that radiation 'Could penetrate right through the human body causing electrical, non-thermal effects, which are capable of long term injury and irreversible damage' (Bentham, 1991, p. 99). Given the present state of knowledge, one might state that although there is cause for concern, the case has yet to be conclusively proven. In other European countries (e.g. Sweden) such a perceived uncertainty is sufficient to imply a real risk to health, so measures are taken to reduce this risk (e.g. encouragement of the use of low emission monitors). In Britain, the attitude taken by authorities such as the Health and Safety Executive is a legalistic one, and seems to be that if a risk cannot be proven, it does not exist. Again, 'The NRPB do not consider that the emissions from a VDU will put either you or your unborn child at risk' (HSE, 1986, p. 1). This could be considered a somewhat cavalier attitude, particularly where young children are concerned.

Many teachers will consider that in a classroom, children rarely experience sustained computer use. The EEC directive states that: 'The employer must plan the worker's activities in such a way that daily work on a display screen is periodically interrupted by breaks or changes of activity' (EEC, 1990, p. 15). At the university where I work, it is considered that significant use covers any employee who uses a computer for more than one hour per day, and that they should take a break from computer use every 45–50 minutes. In a school situation, there are occasions where pupils spend an hour or more at a computer over a piece of work. Where this happens, the teacher has a responsibility to ensure that regular breaks are taken. I would consider any period over half an hour to be sustained use for a child, and they should be given a break from computer use after this time.

Some of the risks related to emissions are not concerned with direct use of the computer but may be caused by passive contact such as sitting next to or behind it. The introduction of the ICT National Curriculum is not going to make these problems go away, indeed it is likely to accentuate them. At present, there are few opportunities for teachers to learn about the risks associated with VDU use and there is no effective checklist in existence for them of which I am aware. Although the National Curriculum for ICT in the Initial Teacher Training consultation document considers that new teachers should know the legal requirements regarding Health and Safety it does not state what those risks are (DfEE, 1998)! This appears to me to be a minimal acknowledgment, as there is no discussion of the nature or cause of such risks. Likewise, pupils' access to computers is not normally monitored to enable the school governors (who have a major role with regard to Health and Safety) to take the problem seriously. One strategy would be for the ICT coordinator to be given time annually to monitor the situation in each room where ICT equipment is installed, and produce a formal report to the governors. This could become a part of the school's ICT policy, and LEAs should offer training in monitoring the use of ICT and workstation analysis for ICT coordinators.

Some of these problems are relatively simple in nature, and simple to cure. In one local school where evidence was gathered recently, a new Acorn Risc PC system had been set up on a purpose-built trolley. The VDU was positioned well above normal head height, even for a tall Year 6 child. This meant that the pupils had to look upwards at quite a steep angle to use the system comfortably. In reality, pupils were observed standing to use the computer, so that the monitor was at a suitable height. This then caused problems with control of the mouse and keyboard on the desk-top, which was situated much lower down. Sustained use of such a system would be likely to induce spinal problems. The solution here would be to move the system off the trolley and place it on a table of the correct height. In another school, the computer was set up on a cupboard with no leg room for the pupils. This meant that they had to sit twisted sideways to use it, forcing them to adopt bad posture. The solution here would be similar.

In a third school, in some classes the computer systems were out of the sight of the teacher because they were placed in a lobby. This meant the teacher had no idea of whether the children were working or not, or when they needed help. The pupils were in Year 2, and they were expected to type in a piece of work, put paper into the printer and print it on their own. They had not been shown how to do this and it led directly to the children becoming frustrated and upset. To avoid such frustrations, the EEC states that 'Software must be easy to use, and . . . adaptable to the operator's level of knowledge' (EEC, 1990, p. 18). This was clearly not the case – the pupils could not use the software effectively without support, which was not given. They were not effectively developing their ICT skills, because they did not know how to use the packages they were given. This was a clear case of ICT giving rise to undue stress and anxiety because of the lack of monitoring and support from the teacher. The solution here would be either to move the computer into the classroom where it could be monitored by the teacher but would not distract the rest of the class, or to ensure a welfare assistant, parent or other helper is briefed to supervise and support the pupils.

According to the EEC, 'All radiation with the exception of the visible part of the electro magnetic spectrum shall be reduced to negligible levels from the point of protection of workers' safety and health' (1990, p. 18). Having read of some concern about the potential hazard caused by emissions from computer monitors, (Hammond, 1986; Branscum, 1990), I undertook measurement of emissions of electro-magnetic emissions in the very low frequency and extremely low frequency ranges, from systems commonly used in local schools. I used a commercially available meter designed for the task. The levels of emission varied considerably between makes and even between different models of the same make. The levels suggested as being safe (by both the Swedish Government and Labour Union) are 2.5 milli gauss for ELF radiation and 0.25 milli gauss for VLF radiation (Taylor, 1993, p. 18). Some of the measurements were well above these recommended safety levels in computer monitors sold by Acorn, Research Machines, Microvitec and Apple, in some cases nearly three times those recommended.

These magnetic emissions are such that they can travel through brick walls. However, the levels of the emissions dropped rapidly with distance away from the computer. At a normal working distance, the measured emissions were minimal. My conclusions from this were that to minimise potential harm, users should sit at least 70 cm (an arm's length) away from the screen, at which distance the emissions were generally negligible and could not be measured. Other pupils should not be allowed to sit either alongside or behind monitors where emission levels can be considerably higher. Low emission monitors are now commonly available, and these should be selected in preference to ordinary monitors.

In addition to the measurement of emissions, screen flicker has also been found to be a factor that causes real distress in some users; I find it so myself. Approximately one in ten of the population is believed to be photo-sensitive, that is, sensitive to flickering lights (Wilkins, 1990). These can cause headaches, visual strain, migraines, and in a small proportion of cases, trigger epileptic fits. 'Between five and twenty out of every 100,000' (Bentham, 1991, p. 93). The combination of fluorescent lighting and computer screens can be particularly unpleasant. I have known a number of students to complain of great discomfort when working with certain systems at the university that have a high level of flicker (Acorn A3000 computers with RGB Philips monitors). Machines manufactured more recently do not suffer to such a great extent from this problem. Having identified this as a hazard, we have managed to reduce the risk by retro-fitting screen guards to reduce the effect of this flicker. This has helped to reduce the discomfort but has not completely removed it. Users of older machines should be aware that screen flicker poses a real hazard to some users. To reduce this hazard, flickering monitors should either be replaced or a screen guard fitted.

Wherever possible, to minimise such problems high refresh rate monitors should be bought and used. (This relates to the speed at which the image on the screen is changed.) Daylight should be used in preference to artificial lighting and screen guards (tinted glass screens that fit over the computer monitor) should be fitted if needed. One added problem here is the movement of the computer industry to Windows-type systems, where the background of the screen is white. This is also a problem with Apple Macintosh and Acorn RISC OS machines. On the older MS DOS systems, the screen display was frequently grey on black, which was much less disturbing to use. Another problem with monitors is that they cause static electrical charges which ionise the air, and can project dust towards the face of the user at high speed when the monitor is switched on. Touching the screen with a finger can give an unpleasant electric shock as the static electricity discharges. This can project any dust at a high speed into the user's face. The static discharges from one computer I used caused the screen guard to swing two centimetres away from vertical when the computer was switched on! A good screen guard, with a cable connected to earth will remove the problem by earthing the discharge.

Practical steps for managing risks

In a school situation, there are two distinct areas to address: first, ensuring safety in the classroom environment, so that pupils, teachers, and non-teaching assistants are not put at risk by the use of ICT; second, ensuring the safety of employees who use ICT in a non-classroom environment – administrative, clerical workers and teachers who use ICT as an administrative tool. Any employee who uses ICT equipment for more that one hour a day should be deemed a regular user and be subject to a workstation analysis to ensure that they are not put at risk from the equipment and furniture. In the classroom, a similar analysis should be undertaken, but with the realisation that the workstation is going to be used by a number of pupils of varying size during the day. It may also be used by a non-teaching assistant, parent or other helper who is brought in to supervise the pupils. Information on undertaking work station analyses can be obtained from the Health and Safety Executive, or from unions representing administrative and technical workers (see Nalgo Safety Representative Newsletter, June 1992).

Based on personal experience of workstations, I would like to make the following suggestions:

- Use a circuit breaker (RCD) with all classroom computer equipment. This will help prevent any risk of injury if there is an electrical malfunction. In a computer lab, this can be built into the mains supply; in a single workstation, it can be incorporated into the mains plug.
- The desks or trolley and chair should be of the correct height for pupils. This is particularly difficult with small children – they should be positioned so that they look down at the screen (which implies the screen being positioned relatively low down). Many trolleys are too high for the pupils they are intended for, and if a monitor is placed on top of a computer processor on a desk of the correct height, the combined height will be too great.
- The chair should provide adequate lumbar support. Ideally a typist's chair with adjustable seat and back should be provided. If that is not possible, a standard classroom chair of the correct height for the table with a supportive back should be used. Stools are not suitable. It may be necessary to provide chairs of different heights to cope with a range of sizes among the children.
- There should be space to place books and papers. This is so that research can be undertaken, sections of documents can be copied into text being processed.
- The screen must be protected from reflections and glare. This may require careful placing of the computer systems, e.g., curtains or blinds over windows to shield screens from direct sunlight.

- Use of non-flicker screens. Older computer screen such as those provided with the BBC computers, produce a disturbing amount of flicker. This can be prevented with modern machines by selecting monitors with a high refresh rate. The effects of flicker, in older monitors, can be reduced by fitting a screen guard. In addition, the use of fluorescent lighting with computer monitors compounds the effects of flicker. In this case, access to indirect daylight is important. No pupil should sit close to VDU, or close to the sides or back to avoid any potential risk from electro-magnetic emissions. An arm's length (70 cms) should be a safe distance for pupils sitting in front of a screen. This should be doubled for children sitting at the sides or to the rear of the VDU. In view of the existence of some tenuous evidence to suggest a risk to unborn babies, it might also be worthwhile recommending that expectant mothers avoid assisting children using ICT.
- Noise must be reduced. This can be done by switching off the internal loudspeaker and providing headphones for computer users. Printing to dot matrix printers should be confined to playtime or times when there is substantial background noise.
- Adequate fresh air ventilation is necessary. This is to overcome the heating and drying effect of computers, and to reduce the ionisation of the air by static electricity. Screen guards that are earthed can also reduce static build-ups on the screen.
- Pupils should not work at a computer for long periods. The visual and physical strain, imposed by concentrating at a computer screen, create real physical problems, even over short periods of time. This might have timetable implications. If a class is time-tabled for a double lesson of ICT, then the teacher should introduce regular breaks in the activity, perhaps moving pupils away from the computers to teach them as a whole class.
- A single computer system should be placed so that its use can be easily monitored. It should be placed as near to the electricity supply as possible, but away from the blackboard (a source of dust) and the sink. Trailing leads and power cables should be kept out of the way so they cannot be interfered with or tripped over. The workstation needs enough room for a group to work at the computer and for them to place books and papers on the table.

Some primary schools have chosen to set up computer labs. When setting up a computer lab, the problems are more complex. A number of machines will exaggerate the problems of noise, heat and other emissions, so adequate ventilation and sound proofing are essential (curtains or blinds at the windows, anti-static carpet on the floor and display boards on the walls). In some teaching rooms mechanical ventilation and air conditioning systems may have to be installed to maintain a satisfactory working environment – but these create noise. The other decision is whether to have the computers placed in rows with the pupils facing the teacher; around the sides of a room (with pupils turned away from the teacher); or in clusters. I have found the preferable arrangement is to teach with computers around the sides of the room. This simplifies constant monitoring of pupils' activities, and regular breaks can be introduced by turning the pupils away from their computers in order to talk to them. The use of computer labs in primary schools might well become more common with the introduction of the Internet. Unless a single Internet connected workstation is required, a networked computer room will probably provide the most cost effective means of providing internet access to a class.

Similar considerations should be undertaken for non-teaching workers using ICT. In particular, the workstation analysis should be undertaken in consultation with the employees concerned. Adequate chairs, desks and workspace should be provided. Some might need footrests. Copy holders will be needed, and the lighting will have to be carefully considered. In this context, it is much cheaper to equip an office workstation satisfactorily than to suffer from possible legal challenges on the grounds of health and safety.

Other associated issues

There are other issues related to health and safety, although not directly caused by computer use. One is the possibility of access to harmful material (e.g. pornography readily accessible from the World Wide Web or communicated by E-Mail). There are software packages available to restrict access to unsuitable material but they do not scan E-Mail. The only way to minimise such risks is for the school to set clear rules preventing access to such materials and to ensure that students know that their access to the Internet is monitored with appropriate sanctions for unsuitable use.

Another is the unsupervised use of ICT rooms by students. This is not in itself a health problem, but the lack of supervision might mean that students are vulnerable. At the University of Exeter, we provide 24-hour open access rooms which are available to students out of teaching hours. In these rooms we have provided a telephone connection to the porter's lodge and they are regularly checked by security staff. Students are only allowed in by a process of signing in at the porter's lodge to acquire a key code for access. We also hope to introduce closed circuit video surveillance to ensure safety both of the students and computer systems. Schools are unlikely to have such problems with 24-hour access, but there is still the problem of supervision of computer rooms and classrooms containing computers in break and lunch times, and after hours. Children should not be left alone, or in groups, without any form of supervision.

All new teachers are required to know about health and safety legislation, and likely hazards to pupils. All serving teachers will also need to know this from the year 2002. Teachers owe a duty of care to their pupils to protect them from unnecessary hazards; they also need to teach them about these hazards, so that pupils do not spend too long working on computers. Until now, such information has not been easily available to schools. Check the computer station in your classroom. Does it offer any hazards in terms of unsuitable furniture, screen flicker, glare or reflections or noise? Can you easily monitor children working on it? How long does each individual or group spend working on it? Are they sufficiently far away from the screen to minimise possible radiation hazard? If the answer to any of these questions is 'no', you need to re-organise the system as a matter of priority to ensure the safety of those in your care.

References

ASSOCIATION OF UNIVERSITY TEACHERS (1998) 'RSI update, health and safety', *Bulletin No 3*.

BAKER, H. (1997) 'Chemical warfare at work', *New Scientist*, **2087**, pp. 30–5.

BENTHAM, P. (1991) *VDU Terminal Sickness*, London: Green Print.

BETTER LIGHTING AT WORK (1992) Lighting Industry Federation, information leaflet.

BRANSCUM, D. (1990) 'The keyboard conundrum', *Macworld*, October, pp. 87–101.

BRODEUR, P. (1990) 'The magnetic field menace', *Macworld*, July, pp. 136–45.

DfEE (1998) *Teaching: High Status, High Standards. Requirements for Courses of Initial Teacher Training* (Circular 4/98), London: TTA Publications.

EEC (1990) Council Directive, *Official Journal of the European Communities*, pp. 156/14 and 156/18.

HAMMOND, C. (1986) 'The hazards of VDUs', *Practical Computing*, June, pp. 73–5.

HEALTH AND SAFETY EXECUTIVE (1986) *Working with VDUs*.

MILLER, N. (1998) 'Air conditioned nightmare', *The Independent on Sunday*, 8 February, pp. 40–1.

NALGO (1992) 'VDU work – new UK regulations', *Safety Representative*.

NUTTALL, N. (1992) 'Are you sitting comfortably?', *The Times*, 18 November.

TAYLOR, C. (1993) 'Electromagnetic emissions from computer monitors', *Computer Education*, **73**, pp. 18–21.

WILKINS, A. (1990) 'Lights can be a health hazard', *Personnel Management Plus*, **1**, No 3, September p. 3.

Chapter 6

Physical education
Carole Raymond

Along with many others, I would argue that there is risk in almost everything we do. Moreover, safety cannot be guaranteed or ensured because unforeseen conditions, improper decisions and poor judgment can all generate risk or hazard. Physical education and its essentially practical element, by its very nature, involves challenge and potential risk. It is recognised as a subject with inherent risk:

> *The value of school sports and physical education is not disputed and there is no suggestion that these activities have to be avoided simply because they carry an inherent risk of injury. However, if an activity is acceptable regardless of its dangers, teachers in charge must minimise those risks by seeing that the activity is carried out in a safe way.* (Croner, 1996, 3–105)

Accepting this, the duty of care requires that teachers will have to make some decisions about the level of acceptable risk and manage any risk involved. As argued above, it does not mean removing the risk. Safety considerations are not intended to restrict the essential practical and challenging nature of physical education but to create and manage a safe learning environment that controls and minimises the risk. The British Association of Advisers and Lecturers in Physical Education (BAALPE) describes this as a *modus operandi*, which identifies all the foreseeable safety problems with activities undertaken in relation to the school curriculum.

> *Common Law and statute law impose general duties on individuals and bodies: Any breach of these duties which causes injury or loss may give rise to a claim for damages (compensation), or sometimes even to criminal penalties. Although accidents will occur because they cannot always be foreseen, teachers*

have a legal duty to work within a system which demonstrates a realistic use of methods which successfully anticipate and eliminate foreseeable risks.

(BAALPE, 1995, p. 21)

This statement alone may generate uneasiness for some teachers, but we must take confidence in much of the good work which currently takes place in primary schools and avoid being too over cautious to the detriment of the subject. It is worth noting that schools do not have an obligation to do the impossible but only to work in a competent and reasonable manner (Gold and Szemerenyi, 1997).

As well as teaching safely, the National Curriculum for Physical Education (NCPE) programme of study and end of Key Stage Descriptions, make reference to pupils learning about safety (DfEE, 1995). Teachers are expected to challenge pupils and to allow them opportunities to work independently. These statutory responsibilities mean that teachers need to develop children's awareness of safety, be able to recognise hazards and assess risks to themselves and others, as well as take responsibility for their own safety and that of others, be they on-site or off-site working in the community. They must also be able to take, suggest or predict appropriate action to control risks such that they can work safely and in accordance with health and safety requirements. This will not just involve children learning about appropriate forms of exercise, the use of various equipment, the safe handling and storage of apparatus, but also that of 'attitudes' towards different codes of conduct, rules and regulations underpinning approved practice in different activity areas. Children need to understand the reasons for adhering to such codes of conduct. All of this relies on the teacher's knowledge, understanding and skills to provide the right experiences. Physical education teachers need to teach safely and teach safety. This means pupils learn safely and learn about safety. This will serve to generate a safety culture and help to ensure legislation becomes active in practice. To help develop teachers' awareness of some of the key issues, this chapter will draw upon further data emerging from a research project conducted in primary schools (NUSAC, 1997)[1] and an analysis of two case reports of alleged negligence.

An increase in the threat of litigation has left many classroom teachers concerned about the potential for accidents in physical education. Data collected from the NUSAC (1997) project, offers some insights into how teachers feel 'increasingly concerned', 'worried', 'uncertain – it is a potential minefield', 'under pressure' and 'vulnerable'. Many are resorting to what are considered 'negligence avoidance' strategies; simply remove the activity and you remove the risk. Comments like 'Far less risky things are undertaken in the gym', 'reluctance to try anything very much' and 'can lead to withdrawal of some activities therefore children lose out', typify this stance. This clearly has implications for the nature of the curriculum offered to pupils. Responses generally indicated that some schools are terrified of being blamed and sued, and are withdrawing involvement in some activities, thus denying opportunities. Swimming, outdoor education and gymnastics apparatus work are the areas under greatest threat.

In Chapter 1, it was recognised that developing a safety culture relies on a number of shareholders playing their part. It requires teachers knowing and understanding their full responsibilities in terms of *duty of care* (see Chapter 1). However, someone must take responsibility to oversee and coordinate the management of health and safety. In most primary schools the head teacher usually delegates formal responsibility for physical education to the subject coordinator. The Teacher Training Agency subject leader qualification reinforces this responsibility as they expect subject leaders to have knowledge and understanding of health and safety requirements (TTA, 1996, p. 10). There is little guidance about what this actually means, but it is likely to include the setting up of a safety policy and risk assessment to reflect the school's policies, and for dissemination among other colleagues (see Chapters 2 and 3). The difficulty here is that the evidence suggests that many physical education coordinators are less experienced staff who are given responsibility for physical education because of their youth and vitality.

In turn, subject coordinators delegate responsibility for the implementation of safety policies to the class teacher, the person at the heart of the learning process. What we must recognise is that many class teachers find physical education a challenging, risky business and they themselves feel uncomfortable, insecure and unsafe with the setting where large groups of children run around in wide open spaces. Some staff feel 'Worried, nervous about letting the children be free', and afraid 'to let the reins go for learning'. It is necessary, therefore, to ensure that teachers feel part of a collective and supportive culture towards safety in their school.

The NUSAC (1997) evidence suggests that teachers are aware of safety issues but not necessarily clued up on the requirements in Physical Education. Of the 136 responses, 60 per cent reported they had a safety policy for physical education. This was made up of very different types of policies: some were separate safety-specific policies; others a safety sub section as part of the general PE policy or externally published policies (see Figure 6.1). This somewhat worrying situation is compounded by the quality of some policies. This varied from detailed information that addressed several general and

FIG 6.1
Key issues identified in
various policies

Procedures	First aid, risk assessment, safety precautions generally (at school and outside school) and specifically for different activities, e.g. swimming, emergency, handling apparatus, jewellery, clothing, etc.
Accident reporting	Procedures and forms
Teaching	Differentiation, SEN, concern for others, progression, class management General guidance and models for good practice, warm ups
Extra curricular	Parental consent forms, transport
Facilities/equipment	Checks and maintenance, handling apparatus.

(NUSAC, 1997)

school specific issues, to those described as 'The BAALPE book' or 'the County guidelines'. The latter suggests that staff do not interact with available literature and use them to design policies to meet their own needs. Other policies tended to focus on accident procedures and first aid rather than management of safety *per se*, thus adopting a reactive rather than proactive approach.

The development of policies in physical education and general issues about safety have been discussed elsewhere (Raymond, 1998). This chapter will therefore attempt to examine teachers' professional, legal and moral responsibilities that determine whether an accident was just that or whether it was an incident involving negligence.

The causes of accidents are numerous but understanding why accidents happen is crucial to managing safe practice and reducing risks. An analysis of accidents by Thomas (1994) revealed a number of similarities contributing to why accidents happen. These range from simple bad luck, poor decision-making, lack of adequate and appropriate group management and supervision to over/under estimation of risk and hazard. Similarly, Hale (1983) and Preist (1996) conclude that most accidents occur when two types of dangers, human and environmental are present and combine at the same time. Ford and Blanchard (1993), argue that it is not the activity which causes accidents but people, by being in the wrong place at the wrong time, with the wrong equipment and/or making wrong decisions. It appears that apart from 'bad luck' and elements outside of our control, there is much teachers and their pupils can do to avoid accidents.

The HSE statistics on page 8 revealed that the majority of major accidents in school occur in games and physical education activities 19.8 per cent, 44.5 per cent in the playground and 3.8 per cent on the school field. I believe there is much to learn from the accidents, experiences and mistakes of others. Two case reports of accidents that occurred in primary physical education lessons will be examined in detail to identify key issues which determined or refuted negligence. In doing this I recognise the importance of reality and how it can be used to raise teachers awareness and inform future practice.

The two cases were selected on the basis of the alleged negligence in two physical education activities in different environments. They offer readers opportunities to draw conclusions on the basis of their legal, professional and moral responsibilities in relation to selected teaching situations and alleged negligence. Such analysis highlights some of the problems teachers face trying to ensure pupils' safety in the learning environment. It is important that the reader tries to remain impartial (see Chapter 1, role of expert witness) and offers a professional opinion based on the facts and the school's duty of care. Conclusions will confirm that the teacher's priority is to work within regular and approved practice even if this leads to some hard decisions in the future. Each case report is presented using the simple format adopted by an expert witness. Having read details of the relevant parties, evidence available and circumstances of the accident, the reader may wish to identify what they consider to be the key issues to be addressed before moving on to compare them with those selected by the expert witness.

Case report I[2]

The relevant parties: The plaintiff (injured party), Rhys, a pupil at Lime Kiln Primary School. The defendant (the local County Council (LCC)), denies negligence.

Evidence available: Individual statements by class teacher Mr C, the head teacher Mrs A and another teacher Mr B; photographs of equipment and layout; and statement of claim and further and better particulars and statement of claim.[3]

Circumstances of the accident: One day in Autumn 1993 Rhys was participating in a gymnastics lesson when he fell from a ladder supported by a fixed and portable apparatus frame and broke his arm. At the time, Rhys was performing what is known as a low impact movement, which involved climbing the apparatus. The medical report indicates that when climbing the ladder Rhys's hands were somewhat slippery and he slipped off the climbing ladder. Rhys claims that he was at the top of the ladder and intended to climb over the top of the frame to the other side. Mr C claims that the general policy is that children do not climb over the top of the frame because of the wires.

Mr C was supervising the lesson. He has a Bachelor of Education degree with qualified teacher status. He has also attended various British Gymnastics Association Courses throughout his 16 years' experience. He is qualified to run a gym club. His statement indicates an awareness of safety issues in the physical education gymnastics lesson.

At the time of the accident, Mr C states he was close to the climbing frame but, as far as he can remember, he was probably looking towards another piece of equipment, the half box. On hearing Rhys fall, Mr C immediately approached him. There were 28 children of similar age and of mixed ability in the class.

Rhys's mother was contacted; she collected her son from school and took him to the general practitioner who referred her to the local Accident and Emergency Department. Rhys was diagnosed as having a green-stick fracture of the shaft of the right ulna. The arm was placed in plaster of paris backslab and he was discharged. The plaster was later replaced with a complete above elbow plaster. This was removed a month later and he returned to school and normal sports after the Christmas vacation.

The issues to be addressed: Rhys alleges negligence on the basis that there were insufficient mats and inadequate supervision by the teacher. Both of these points will involve examining the nature of the activity.

Before moving on to the next section, you might like to make a note of the issues which you think are relevant in determining whether the teacher was negligent or not. What questions would a judge ask to assess whether 'reasonable' care was provided? What texts would you consider to define regular and approved practice?

The facts on which the expert's opinion is based:

The activity was appropriate to the curriculum for this age group. It is common practice for pupils to work on apparatus that requires them to climb, move along, and over, onto and off (Physical Education in the National Curriculum 1992). Pupils were engaged in experimental learning and use of the apparatus. This is recognised as the 'indirect' approach to teaching gymnastics (BAALPE, 1990, p. 33). This approach allows children to approach the exercises that have been set in their own way. Furthermore, the individualism of response to the tasks set makes the system of catching and 'standing by' which is absolutely essential in the direct approach, almost unusable in this approach (p. 40).

The County Council Policy Statement, section 3, offers guidelines for Teaching and Learning strategies. Section 3.1 refers to safe practice and states that wherever the organisation and standards of safety have become part of the pupils accepted patterns of behaviour, it would be appropriate to employ as wide a range of teaching styles and learning strategies as possible to suit the varied abilities and rates of progression within the normal class. Section 3.2 continues that within the range of activities taught, some will lend themselves more to experiential and experimental methods of learning (e.g., dance, creative gymnastics). This approach is evident in the statement provided by Mr C.

Mr C states that working on the apparatus was not a new activity for the class and that they would have been familiar with safety requirements. There is evidence of the National Curriculum requirements in Mr C's statement regarding lesson content and his approach to safety.

The apparatus was in good condition and appropriate for this activity and for use at Key Stage 1 and 2. The photographs reveal it is standard equipment for a primary school gymnasium/hall. The school has a selection of gymnastics equipment including six mats. There are no 'crash' mats.

All teachers would be expected to make safety checks on the condition of the fixed and portable apparatus and the mats to be used in the lesson. Furthermore, the teacher would be responsible for making judgments on the height and appropriateness of the apparatus and the layout of any mats to be used in relation to pupil needs.

There were no mats immediately around the equipment. The British Association of Advisers and Lecturers in Physical Education, *Safe Practice in Physical Education* (1990)[4] text is considered one of the key manuals to be used by all teachers of physical education, whatever their experience. It is recognised by Institutions of Physical Education as an important reference text for initial teacher education courses and is acknowledged by the Department of Education and Employment. The statement on the safety of apparatus (pp. 36–7) includes a detailed section on mats with a number of points for consideration. Two points are offered in relevance to this case:

- matting of sufficient size and density should be placed wherever needed
- the mat should not produce excessive recoil. Recoil can cause excessive stress on joints, especially the ankles, and can cause the gymnast to fall and exacerbate any injury.

There is no formal prescriptive statement indicating that mats should be placed around certain types of apparatus and no reference to 'crash' mats.

The British Amateur Gymnastics Association Teachers Award Primary Sector syllabus is a relatively new document, but the guidance for safety clearly states, under apparatus placement, that mats should be considered as pieces of apparatus not landing areas (p. 7). The school policy clearly states that physical education mats are not intended as a safety measure but as a piece of apparatus in their own right. This corresponds with the County Curriculum Policy statement section 6. Mr C's statement reflects awareness and understanding of this policy.

Supervision and the staff:pupil ratio was within normal conditions. When pupils are engaged in experiential and experimental learning, it is not unusual for the teacher to be moving around the gymnasium/hall. Mr C would not be expected to directly support Rhys as he had no special needs and had previously engaged in similar activities with confidence and competence.

In preparing the pupils for the activity, the teacher would be expected to conduct a warm up prior to activity on the apparatus, provide instructions and/or demonstration of the expectations during the lesson, and maintain adequate supervision of the class throughout the lesson. The teacher should have knowledge of the subject and its aims, of young people and their development, and be a skilful observer.

Physical education has inherent challenges and risks built into the subject. The caring teacher offers the subject and minimises the risks within standard and nationally accepted practice. The task set for Rhys, and others in his class, was within that practice.

Teachers would be expected to be familiar with regular and approved practice according to guidance offered in BAALPE (1990) Safe Practice in Physical Education and additional LEA guidelines, as appropriate. The school documentation does reflect evidence of these specific texts.

The expert's conclusion

The circumstances in which Rhys fell and sustained injury did not put him at risk. The climbing activity in which he was engaged is not an activity with a high associated level of danger or risk. It is recognised as appropriate at Key Stage 2 – pupils up to 11 years of age.

The apparatus used meets specified requirements and was safely assembled. The use of mats would not necessarily have prevented or reduced injury received by a person falling from any height. The use of mats around apparatus of this type can occasionally prove more dangerous and increase any level of risk as they can encourage children to be over-adventurous and jump from inappropriate heights. On no account would 'crash' mats or high recoil mats be used as these often provide excessive recoil and exacerbate injury. They also encourage children to take more risks.

The task of exploring apparatus is appropriate at this Key Stage. There is some discrepancy about instructions to climb over the top of the climbing frame. Mr C statement denies such instruction. It is my opinion that it is unlikely children would specifically be told to do this.

The Curriculum Policy statement provided by the county, and health and safety statement provided by the school, both indicate an awareness of the need for safe practice in physical education. These documents reflect standard practices adopted by many other counties in England. These policies reflect National Curriculum Orders and the safe practice guidance provided by BAALPE.

It is normal standard practice for a teacher to be 'circulating' giving pupils individual assistance. With a class of 28 pupils I would not have expected Mr C to place himself beside Rhys for any or all of their group activity on the ladder. The only reason for doing this would be in the case of a child with special needs. Rhys was not identified as having a special need. The level of supervision provided by the teacher during the gymnastics apparatus work was acceptable and reasonable.

The activity was not of a high risk nature and well within the capabilities of Rhys. The expert did not regard it as hazardous enough to require direct supervision or support. To conclude, the professional opinion regarded the activity as acceptable, within a controlled apparatus environment, with sound supervision where an unfortunate accident happened. *No negligence.*

A similar case is reported in Croner's the Head's Legal Guide and judicial comment and approval of 'indirect' or 'modern educational thought' in movement teaching is evident. In *Freigate v. Middlesex County Council (1954)* a 6-year-old girl attending infant school was engaged in recreational exercises. The girl, sitting on a low horizontal bar, 3 ft 6 in off the floor, fell and broke her left arm. Her parents claimed damages and alleged that there was neither individual or adequate supervision by the teacher concerned, it being admitted that she, although standing near to the bars, was attending to a small boy who had climbed up a step ladder. It was held that no liability fell upon the LEA.

Case report 2

The relevant parties: The plaintiff, Amanda, a pupil at Woodstock Primary School. The defendant, the Local County Council (LCC), denies negligence.

Evidence available: A copy of Amanda's statement dated August 1995 and a site report on the playing field condition at Woodstock School dated October 1995.

(Preparation of the report involved reference to a number of texts documented in Appendix 6.1 at the end of this chapter.)

Circumstances of the accident: One afternoon in summer 1987 Amanda was participating in an outdoor athletics lesson. Along with other pupils she was working on the Milk Awards and trying to qualify for different badges of various grades. The accident happened when Amanda was performing the running 'test' on the grass playing area, when she fell and injured her leg. Mr F, the teacher in charge of the lesson, examined Amanda's knee and carried her to the first aid room. She was later taken by taxi to the local hospital where a four-hour operation was performed on her knee. The injury sustained by Amanda may affect her career and long-term involvement in activity.

At the time of the accident there were two classes working on the field and the approximately 60 pupils were being supervised by two teachers, Mr F and Ms R.

The issues to be addressed: Amanda alleges her foot became stuck in a small pothole, that the maintenance of the track was poor with many changes in level and many surface blemishes. The suitability and condition of the playing field is alleged as unsafe.

What are the issues for you in this quite different case? Once again you might like to identify what you consider to be the key issues upon which negligence can be proven. Remember – you must focus on regular and approved practice and reasonable duty of care.

The facts on which the expert's opinion is based:

The facilities: It is not unusual for pupils to be involved in running activities on the school playing fields that at different times of the year may be used for different activities. There is no exact evidence to show that the playing area did contain small potholes. What is clear is that Amanda tripped on something and fell and injured herself.

LCCs and schools have a have a duty to provide a safe learning environment for their pupils (HSW Act, 1974). This requires the teacher in charge to inspect the playing field, running area, and make a decision on its suitability for use. If there were any concerns about the suitability of the working area, the teacher would be expected to report any damage, repair any damage, or take the facility out of use. This would clearly indicate that the teacher was undertaking risk assessment, risk monitoring and risk minimising (see Chapter 3). It is normal practice for facilities to be monitored and maintained annually. There are no records to indicate that this actually happened at the school.

Schools, and in turn teachers, must work in accordance with regular and approved practice regarding the upkeep and maintenance of facilities. At the time of the accident, this included guidance and recommendations provided by BAALPE (1990), Amateur Athletics Association (AAA), English Schools Athletics Association (ESAA) and the local education authority in which the school is located. At the time of the accident BAALPE recommended a safety code for teachers of athletics

> ❦ *Only undertake the coaching of athletic events and activities when you are sure that . . . the layout of facilities, class organisation and apparatus being used can in no way be faulted.* (p. 67)

The playing field report suggests that safety is not a high priority at the school now. 'Obviously many of the defects are long-standing and have been left unattended.' . . . 'Undulations in the playing surface, while appearing relatively innocent probably carry with them a greater risk of injury.' It is not unreasonable to assume that the condition of the field did heighten the risk for accident in 1987.

Supervision: Risk assessment serves to minimise the risk inherent in physical education activities. There is no evidence to suggest that this took place. While the quality of supervision regarding class control and discipline is not disputed, the level of supervision regarding where pupils were working in relation to the quality of the field area is questionable. This is no doubt a difficult area, as teachers often feel pressurised to work in environments that do not always meet safety regulations. However, where a teacher feels the employer is not fulfilling their responsibilities, to provide adequate, well-maintained facilities, then it would be prudent for the teacher to adopt recognised good practice common elsewhere in the education system and, following a risk assessment, refuse to use the area. It is not uncommon for teachers to take this action given their responsibility for a duty of care towards their pupils.

The expert's conclusion

In hot summers, holes can appear in grass surfaces which make the surface uneven. Solutions have to be found to make such areas safe via risk assessment. Some teachers have been known to refuse to teach on unsafe playing fields until maintenance has been undertaken. By not showing evidence of risk assessment of the state of the playing fields, Amanda along with other pupils were put at risk of injury. It would appear that the school did not prioritise maintenance and monitoring of its facilities and in turn heightened the risk.

Amanda was too young to share in the decision-making about the running surface, whereas an older pupil would have recognised the unsafe nature of the track. The accident was clearly one which should have been avoided. The expert opinion is that there was clear evidence of negligence and a clear breach of the duty of care.

Lessons to be learned

What can be learned from these two contrasting cases? No doubt you have drawn some of your own conclusions and in doing so have started to consider your responsibilities within the reality of the work place. In both cases the key issues for teachers were quality of facility and the level of supervision, which are inextricably linked to the nature of the activity. When examining evidence, it is not unusual for teachers to try to locate the accident in a particular situation, for example, 'Yes, but if we didn't use the field . . .' or, 'but boys will be boys', but what is important is that teachers should have already considered this in their risk assessment and taken adequate measures to remove the risk.

Facilities: We all know that some of our facilities are not up to standard. This was evident during the three-year OFSTED inspection cycle of secondary schools that recently reported serious deficiencies in some schools while recognising that others, which shared community facilities, enjoyed outstandingly good, effectively-managed and well-maintained accommodation (1998, p. 158). If this is the situation in secondary schools offering specialist physical education, what can we expect in primary schools? A review of inspection findings 1993/94 concluded that the poorest accommodation is often outdoors and suffers in the main from poor drainage and/or adequate maintenance. In some cases poor surfaces render conditions unsafe (1995, p. 4). The report suggests as a key issue for all schools is the systematic attention that needs to be given to the maintenance of facilities – especially playing fields and outdoor hard play areas – and the inspection of gymnastics equipment (p. 6). A more recent report of standards in primary physical education concluded:

❜ *Resources are generally adequate, but the need to renew expensive gymnastics mats or apparatus is beyond the budget of some schools. In the majority of schools, accommodation is adequate, but in a significant minority of schools the lack of a school hall, deteriorating hard areas, sloping fields or poor drainage restrict proper development of physical education.* (OFSTED, 1998, p. 2)

A similar but graver situation is reported in Wales:

❜ *In general, there is sufficient specialist accommodation to teach the NC, but some is in poor condition ... difficulties are ... often the result of poor maintenance.* (OHMCI, 1997, p. 14)

This extends to the quality of the playing fields:

❜ *Grassed playing fields vary in quality and condition but are satisfactory in two-thirds of the schools at least for part of the year. Poor drainage often renders parts unusable for extensive periods during winter months. Maintenance services are often inadequate and delays in grass cutting and marking of pitches occur frequently ... Some facilities present hazards: the provision for cricket is often poor, and many pitches are not sufficiently maintained for the game to be played safely.*

Given that running tracks usually double up as the playing boundary for cricket, it is safe to say that fields generally could be considered unsafe.

Interestingly, the report does not target the quality of facilities and accommodation in its list of conclusion and issues for attention. In a later report focusing on standards and quality in primary schools' physical education and sport, one of the main findings concluded

> *2.11 Deficiencies in accommodation and resources adversely affect the quality of educational provision and standards of pupils' achievements in many primary schools.*
>
> *The difficulties tend to be most acute in small schools.*   (OHMCI, 1998, p. 3)

The report discusses substantial shortcomings in the facilities available (p. 16). However, once again in the 10 key issues for action, all but one point relates to what schools and teachers have to do. The exception is the issue of improving the quality of accommodation and it begins with the need to eliminate large classes. There is no recognition of the government's responsibility for ensuring facilities are of good quality. Surely schools cannot address the issue of poor accommodation on their own. What message does this offer, that safety is not important if it costs money? It is time for teachers to begin to work within their legal and professional responsibilities and this means refusing to allow their pupils to work in substandard accommodation. By ignoring the key issues they are not only putting the children at risk but themselves too.

Supervision: It is not unusual for 'lack of supervision' or 'inadequate supervision' to be cited in a negligence claim. Teachers supervisory duties include the effective and efficient management of pupils to minimise the potential for negligent actions.

In Figure 6.2 BAALPE (1995) offers guidance on the nature of supervision that pupils should receive when participating in curriculum and extra-curricular activities. When analysed most of the guidance relates to areas such as knowing your pupils' needs, understanding the environment and providing appropriate experience. However, in some cases, teachers have been found lacking because they failed to adequately train, inform, and supervise the pupils. Wyness (1989) considers the use of the phrase *quality and quantity of supervision*, so often found in American legal briefs.

> *Quality implies a degree of ability to supervise greater than might be expected from an average citizen. This implies a level of expertise commensurate with the complexity and risk associated with the activity and it might include the expectancy of licensing, certification, credentials, and/or appropriate experience. Quantity of supervision refers to the number of supervisors assigned to*

Teachers should ensure that the following requirements are met:

a All pupils should know what is expected of them.

b The size of any teaching group should be modified according to the maturity, competence, intelligence and experience of the pupils and the nature of the activities in which they are involved.

c Teachers in Northern Ireland and Scotland should refer to regulations on nationally agreed class sizes.

d Teachers should know of any individual needs and strengths of pupils. A teacher's awareness of any special educational needs, disabilities or medical conditions of pupils has often been significant in cases of negligence considered by the courts.

e Teachers should be aware of any drug treatment, which a pupil may be receiving and take account of its known effects on the sensory perception, motor control and coordination of the pupil.

f Special safety precautions in determining the appropriate nature and level of an activity will be necessary when a pupil is inexperienced, immature, has a disability or demonstrates a behaviour disorder.

g Class numbers should be checked through registration at the start of a lesson. In swimming and cross-country running, counting checks should be made at the beginning and the end of activity.

h Wherever possible, younger pupils should be accompanied on journeys to and from inter-school matches played at venues other than at their own school and should otherwise be organised to travel as a group. Parental consent should be obtained when direct supervision on such occasions cannot be provided.

(BAALPE, 1995, p. 38)

the activity. The number of participants, the area in which the activity is taking place, and the degree of risk associated with the activity are the deter-mining factors in establishing the appropriate number of supervisors. An additional concern should be the age and experience of those engaging in the activity, and the possibility of rowdy or reckless behaviour. The greater the potential for problems, the greater the need for an increase in the quality and the quantity of supervisors.

It is recognised that quality and quantity are not to be seen as mutually exclusive terms, but that they should both be kept in mind when structuring PE programmes. In the gymnastics case, the teacher had clearly provided a good quality of supervision in that the activity developed previous experience, apparatus was appropriate and pupils were instructed and carefully observed during the lesson. The teacher was not expected to be everywhere at once and, because of the style of teaching employed, the level of supervision was acceptable in line with approved practice. In the case of the running, a low risk activity, general supervision of the pupils was not in question, but the specific supervision of the workplace was inadequate. Inasmuch as facilities exist throughout the entire year, it is virtually impossible to have 24-hour surveillance, but supervision must be provided at times of usage. The teacher should have been aware of the damage to the work surface, via risk assessment, and taken the necessary action – this may simply have involved using another area of the field.

This is a particularly sensitive issue for many teachers, as they will argue that poor facilities are often out of their control and not to use them would further reduce the activities to be offered. Nevertheless they do have a duty to report 'inadequate' facilities to management and to take appropriate action. Given the increase in litigation, risks can be costly and at the end of the day, the teachers have to show that they made a professional judgment based on regular and approved practice.

What is regular and approved practice in physical education?

During the preparation of an expert report, witnesses will seek to identify what is approved, standard or common practice in a subject area at the time of the accident. Physical education is perhaps more complicated than many areas as it has six quite different activity areas, the majority of which are linked to sport in society. They are therefore not only guided by professional associations linked with physical education, e.g. BAALPE and PEA UK, but also National Governing Bodies in Sport. So, the more complex the issue, the greater the source of reference. In the case of the gymnastics accident, the BAGA materials were consulted because the use of mats and different types of teaching approaches are regularly questioned in primary schools. In contrast, the running accident was a straightforward activity caused by the teacher's lack of risk assessment. What makes this issue more complicated is the fact that teachers often feel maintenance and facility issues are 'out of their control'. Clearly they are not, for there are precautions that could and should have been taken. This is reinforced in the OFSTED findings which are also contributory texts used to define regular and approved practice.

Conclusions

The two quite different case reports were carefully selected to illustrate that it is not the activity which causes the accident but the result of a number of circumstances coming together. Hindsight is a wonderful thing and at times, on reflection, teachers may conclude that the combination of events may have been foreseeable or predictable. When all is said and done, a teacher has to try to ensure that as far as is possible they have provided a reasonable duty of care within their legal, professional and moral responsibilities. Where teachers themselves feel at risk it is their personal responsibility to raise this with senior staff, coordinators, head teachers and governors, who in turn have a duty to take action. This will help generate a working culture in which physical education will continue to offer both teachers and pupils risk and challenge in safety.

Notes

1. NUSAC 1997 refers to a survey conducted in schools across the south west. The data is used to illustrate teachers concerns. A full report is in preparation to be published at a later date.
2. The names of the plaintiff and the defendants have been changed to protect confidentiality.
3. Preparation of the report involved reference to a number of texts, these are usually documented at the back of the report and give some insight into published material used to endorse regular and approved practice. To avoid repetition materials used in both cases report examples is referenced in Appendix 6.1.
4. When offering a professional opinion it is normal practice for an expert to make reference to the texts in existence at the time of the accident.

References

BAALPE (1995) *Safe Practice in Physical Education*, Dudley: Dudley LEA.

CRONER (1996a) *The Head's Legal Guide*, Kingston-upon-Thames: Croner Publications.

CRONER (1996b) *The Teacher's Legal Guide*, Kingston-upon-Thames: Croner Publications.

DfEE (1995) *National Curriculum for Physical Education*, London: HMSO.

FORD, P. and BLANCHARD, J. (1993) *Leadership and Administration of Outdoor Pursuits*, PA: Venture Publishing Inc.

GOLD, R. and SZEMERENYI, S. (1997) *Running a School: Legal Duties and Responsibilities: 1998*, Bristol: Jordans.

HALE, A. (1983) *Safety Management for Outdoor Programme Leaders*, Unpublished Manuscript.

NUSAC (1997) Research project (phase 1) investigating current policy and practice towards safe practice in primary schools across the South West. Final report in press.

OFSTED (1995) *Physical Education: A Review of Inspection Findings*, London: HMSO.

OFSTED (1998) *Secondary Education 1993–97, A Review of Secondary Schools in England*, London: The Stationery Office.

OHMCI (1997) *Standards and Quality in Primary Schools Physical Education and Sport*, Cardiff: Hackman Print.

OHMCI (1998) *Standards and Quality in Secondary Schools Physical Education and Sport*, Cardiff: Hackman Print.

PREIST, S. (1996) 'Thoughts on managing dangers in adventure programmes', *Journal of Adventure Education and Outdoor Leadership*, **13**, (1), pp. 18–21.

RAYMOND, C. W. (1998) *Coordinating Physical Education Across the Primary School*, London: Falmer Press.

TEACHER TRAINING AGENCY (1996) *Consultation Papers on Standards and a National Professional Qualification for Subject Leaders*, London: HMSO.

THOMAS, S. M. (1994) 'Adventure education: Risk and safety out of school', in S. M. THOMAS (ed.) *Outdoor Education*, Perspectives, 50: University of Exeter.

WYNESS (1989) 'Effective supervision of movement programs', in *JOPERD*, January, pp. 65–8.

Appendix 6.1

BAALPE (1985) *Safe Practice in Physical Education*, Chester: BAALPE.

BAALPE (1990) *Safe Practice in Physical Education*, Leeds: White Line Press.

BAALPE (1995) *Safe Practice in Physical Education*, Dudley: Dudley LEA.

DES (1992) *National Curriculum in Physical Education*, London: HMSO.

THE BRITISH AMATEUR GYMNASTICS ASSOCIATION *Teachers Award Primary Sector*, Resource Materials: unpublished.

SITE INSPECTION REPORT (1995) (including photographs) GS Services.

Chapter 7

Safety issues in science

Nigel Skinner

> ❝ *Safety awareness in general, and during science activities in particular, is an essential attitude to be developed in young children and one which can be applied and extended throughout their lives.* (Raper and Stringer, 1987, p. 125)

The introduction of the National Curriculum in 1989 formalised the position of science in primary schools and many aspects of biological and physical science are now part of the core curriculum. Learning about many of these is often best achieved through practical activities and *Science in the National Curriculum* (DFE, 1995) promotes an experimental and investigative approach to the teaching and learning of all aspects of science. As a consequence, practical science activities in primary schools are often open ended and, to help them learn about scientific methods, pupils should also be given opportunities to carry out investigations that they have planned themselves. Clearly, such practical and investigative approaches must not put pupils at unnecessary risk and when planning science activities teachers need to consider their duty of care and minimise the possibility of pupils coming to any harm. Additionally, the National Curriculum requires teachers to develop pupils' safety awareness by providing opportunities to recognise risks and act appropriately. Clearly, this can only be done if pupils participate in activities that involve some degree of risk. This chapter discusses these contrasting demands in the light of teachers' legal liabilities and suggests approaches that could be used when formulating a science safety policy and a curriculum to develop pupils' safety awareness.

Accidents and litigation related to school science

Fortunately very few serious accidents related to science activities in the primary school have been reported in the literature. Borrows (1997) reports one accident that involved a group of children working with hot water. They were comparing the rate at which hot water cooled when it was placed in containers made of different types of material. Hot water was poured into a thin polystyrene cup, the heat caused the cup to collapse and a pupil was scalded by the hot water. Two obvious and simple lessons can be learned from this incident – procedures and apparatus should always be checked before using them with pupils and practical work in science must be supervised closely at all times. There is no evidence of primary schools being prosecuted for breaches of Health and Safety legislation relating to the teaching of science, however, a number of secondary school teachers have been prosecuted following incidents that have caused injury to pupils in science lessons. In each of these cases the teachers involved had failed to take reasonable safety precautions when carrying out practical work that was known to be hazardous. A secondary school has also been fined £7,000 and ordered to pay over £1,000 in costs following an incident at an open evening in which two pupils were injured as a result of an explosion that occurred when they were making sparklers. In this case the school rather than an individual teacher was fined because it did not have procedures in place to ensure that its safety policy was implemented.

The fact that so few accidents and prosecutions are known to have occurred during primary science activities is testament to the practice employed by primary teachers to plan their activities very carefully and be vigilant and professional in their approach. Nevertheless, more teachers are now responsible for delivering the science statutory Orders and there is evidence that some parents, whose children are injured in school, now seek someone to blame. Many even look for negligence as a means of compensation. To refute negligence teachers will need to provide evidence that they are fulfilling their responsibilities (see Part 1) and that they provide a safe learning environment as normal routine practice.

Health and safety legislation relevant to primary science

Science as a core subject in the curriculum means that virtually every class teacher is involved in science activities and there is a need for existing knowledge and awareness of health and safety to be spread more widely and to become established in routine practice. With the increase in safety legislation and development of a 'compensation culture' as discussed in Chapter 1, it is also important that primary teachers plan and teach practical science in compliance with current safety legislation. All teachers work within the framework of both common and statute law. Under common law teachers have a *duty of care* when acting *in loco parentis*. In this context all practical work in science must be carried out with due regard for pupils' health and safety. This, coupled with a number of statutes, has implications for the teaching of practical science. The main Act of Parliament relevant in this context is the Health and Safety at Work Act (1974). This Act is an example of enabling legislation. This means that, under the Act, parliament is permitted to introduce new health and safety regulations and a variety of such regulations that need to be considered in the context of primary science have emerged.

The *Control of Substances Hazardous to Health (COSHH) Regulations (1989)* were introduced to protect employees and others from substances that might be hazardous to health. The hazardous substances covered by these regulations include those that are classified as toxic, harmful, corrosive or irritant, harmful micro-organisms and substantial quantities of dust. The packaging in which toxic, harmful, corrosive or irritant substances are sold carries warning symbols that indicate the potential dangers associated with their use. It is worth noting that some household substances that are easily obtainable from shops (e.g. bleach, disinfectants, dishwasher detergents and powders for automatic washing machines) carry these warnings and should not be handled by pupils. If practical work in science involves hazardous substances then to comply with the COSHH regulations a risk assessment must be carried out and steps taken to control any risks that have been identified and thus minimise the chances of harm being caused. The Health and Safety Commission recommend that educational employers adopt the principle of requiring that model, or general risk assessments, are consulted by teachers to find out about restrictions or precautions that need to be observed when using hazardous substances. The guidance that is 'accepted by almost all education employers as providing model risk assessments for activities in primary science' (Qualification and Curriculum Authority, 1998, p. 11) can be found in *Be Safe! Some Aspects of Safety in School Science and Technology for Key Stages 1 and 2* (Association for Science Education (ASE) 1990) referred to below as *Be Safe!* Borrows (1997) similarly claims this to be the text used in most UK primary schools. It has a very accessible style and contains essential advice concerning safe procedures to be used when teaching primary science. A separate Scottish edition (ASE, 1995) provides guidance for the Scottish environmental studies 5–14 curriculum.

The study of living organisms may pose health risks and details of the laws relating to the study and care of living things in schools are set out in Administrative memorandum 3/90 *Animals and Plants in Schools: Legal aspects* (DES, 1990). Much of this legislation is concerned with preventing ill-treatment of animals (e.g. The Protection of Animals Act, *1911*) or the conservation of wildlife (e.g. The Wildlife and Countryside Act, *1981*). However, other aspects of the legislation have very clear health and safety implications. The Dangerous Wild Animals Act *(1976)* makes it illegal to keep many species of wild animals in schools (including all monkeys and apes, members of the crocodile and alligator family and poisonous snakes). There are a number of diseases that can be transmitted from animals to humans and for this reason the Health and Safety at Work Act *(1974)* places restrictions on keeping certain animals in schools. For example, animals which should not be kept include mammals and birds caught in the wild (some of these may carry the bacterium which causes Weil's disease), terrapins and tortoises (which can carry *Salmonella*) and recently imported Giant African land snails (which may harbour a lung parasite that can infect humans). Children often bring injured mammals or birds into schools and since these may be infected they should be removed from the premises as quickly as possible. Animal welfare organisations such as the RSPCA will provide advice on the best course of action to take. Any dead animals are also likely to be infected and should be put into a plastic bag and placed in a rubbish bin. *Be Safe!* provides examples of animals which are suitable for keeping in schools and guidance on all aspects of their care.

The Management of Health and Safety at Work Regulations (MHSW) (1992) extend the principle of risk assessment that was introduced with the COSHH Regulations to cover any activity that involves some degree of risk, not simply those involving substances hazardous to health. For example, in primary science this would include activities such as pond dipping and other types of fieldwork, off-site visits and heating or burning things in the classroom. Before involving pupils in these types of activities a risk assessment should be conducted in consultation with available guidance. However, the main purpose of the MHSW is to ensure that employers set up monitoring systems to check that agreed procedures are actually being implemented. This means that educational employers must make arrangements for the planning, organisation, control, monitoring and review of safety management. In practice, responsibility for these at the subject level is usually delegated to the subject coordinators and, to comply with the legislation, subject policies should include reference to health and safety issues.

FIG 7.1
References to safety in science in the National Curriculum (1995)

The introduction to the Key Stage 1 and 2 programmes of study (often referred to as Sc0) in the current version of Science in the National Curriculum (Department for Education, 1995) includes statements under the heading 'Health and Safety' which apply across the whole of the science curriculum.

At Key Stage 1, it states that pupils should be given opportunities to:
a) recognise hazards and risks when working with living things and materials;
b) follow simple instructions to control the risks to themselves.

At Key Stage 2, pupils should be given opportunities to:
a) recognise and assess the hazards and risks to themselves and to others when working with living things and materials;
b) take action to control these risks.

Science in the National Curriculum (DFE, 1995, p. 2 and p. 7)

National curriculum science orders and initial teacher training

As previously mentioned, to meet Health and Safety requirements class teachers must understand and apply the principles of risk assessment and follow regular and approved practice. If pupils are to become responsible, safety conscious adults, they too need to learn how to assess and control risks. This is an essential requirement of the *National Curriculum Science Orders* (DFE, 1995) that require teachers to promote in pupils a sense of personal responsibility for health and safety in the context of science (see Figure 7.1). Furthermore, changes to teacher training courses (DFE Circular, 14/93) mean that schools now assume greater responsibility for the training of prospective teachers and therefore need to ensure that trainees receive appropriate opportunities to develop specific areas of knowledge and understanding as identified in the ITT Standards (see Figure 7.2).

Clearly, schools involved in initial teacher training will need to teach trainees how to teach and manage science activities that take account of the safety and legal considerations. Schools that have a safety culture with an effective safety policy for science will be in a stronger position to fulfil this requirement than schools in which no such policy exists.

Devising a primary science safety policy

All schools need a safety policy if they are to comply with health and safety legislation. The findings of a small-scale study carried out by the author in

FIG 7.2
ITT requirements for
courses in primary
science

Curriculum guidelines for ITT courses in primary science. This requires all primary trainees to be taught how to teach and manage science activities and take account of safety and legal considerations, including:

- the potential hazards associated with teaching the science content of Programmes of Study at KS1 and KS2 and how to avoid these hazards;
- assessing the risks associated with particular science activities and how to select a safe way to proceed, e.g. *melting substances using a hotplate, a candle in a sand tray or hot water as the heat source*;
- how to teach pupils to recognise risks and act safely;
- current legislation relevant to teaching science at KS1 and KS2, e.g. *care of living things, keeping animals in the classroom.*

Trainees must also demonstrate that they know and understand health and safety requirements and how to implement them, including:

- the major legal requirements for health and safety, including restrictions on keeping living things in the classroom;
- the fact that every activity involves an element of risk which should be assessed and allowed for in planning and organising it;
- the accepted actions and procedures in the event of an accident.

(DfEE Circular, 4/98 – *Teaching: High Status, High Standards*, 1998, p. 75, p. 80)

1998 suggests that many primary science coordinators would welcome guidance to help them formulate a safety policy for primary science. Seven primary science coordinators were interviewed. Two worked in first schools (age range 4–8 years), three in primary schools (age range 4–11), one in a junior school (age range 7–11) and one in a middle school (age range 8–12). The middle school science coordinator was the only one who had received INSET training concerning safety in science and this was the only school in which an appropriate science safety policy was in place. As expected, the main source of information regarding safety issues in primary science (used by six of the seven schools) was *Be Safe!* and all schools were aware of the need to plan practical science activities with health and safety issues in mind. However, there was a mistaken belief that this booklet constituted an acceptable science policy. While the guidance is appropriate and valuable, it can only contribute to the implementation of a policy.

> *. . . A safety policy is not a statement of all the ways in which practical science activities are to be carried out . . . Rather, it defines procedures and areas of responsibility, in order to promote safe working for staff and pupils alike.*

(Borrows, 1993, p. 133)

A policy is an important form of communication within a school that sets out procedures and areas of responsibility that will promote and monitor safe working practices for both teachers and pupils, taking account of their particular circumstances. Vincent and Borrows (1992) suggest that a science safety policy would normally contain the following sections:

- An introduction outlining the importance of safety issues in science
- Specific responsibilities of particular staff
- General responsibilities of all staff
- Procedures
- Regular checks
- Pupils
- A list of safety resources.

The introduction

This should set the scene and emphasise that legislation requires schools to have a general safety policy and as there are particular safety concerns associated with practical science it is sensible to have a specific policy relating to science. It should also stress that it is the responsibility of all those involved in teaching science (including classroom assistants and voluntary helpers) to implement the safety policy and follow approved procedures. This will include:

- Planning practical work and fieldwork such that it controls and minimises hazards
- Always using safe procedures to achieve the desired educational objectives. This does not mean avoiding all aspects of risk, but to manage risk so that pupils experience and learn to identify and control risks themselves
- Reporting any concerns
- Recognition of other guidance available and used, e.g. *Be Safe!* and LEA guidelines.

Specific responsibilities

As the person to whom overall responsibility for science in the school has been delegated, the science coordinator would normally be expected to ensure that:

- The safety policy is kept up-to-date and that all those involved in teaching science are aware of its importance and follow the guidelines it contains
- All science resources that are used are safe and appropriate. For example, this would include consulting model risk assessments regarding any animals that may be kept in the school and the equipment and chemicals that are used in science lessons

- Science resources that may pose a risk to pupils are stored securely and safely
- Information about safety issues in primary science are disseminated to all the relevant people
- All those involved in science activities are aware of and follow regular and approved practice. Tawney (1992) argues that the most effective way of doing this is to include details of relevant safety precautions in schemes of work, lesson plans, pupil texts and worksheets. Doing this will bring safety information to 'point-of-use-texts' where it will be seen by all those involved in either planning or carrying out practical science activities
- All staff are involved in the monitoring and evaluation of practice and in policy and procedures being updated and communicated to all concerned. This will include the identification of any INSET needs.

General responsibilities

All those involved in planning and teaching science share responsibility for:
- Implementing the agreed policy in their own classrooms. They will need to ensure that they instruct and supervise their classes in accordance with approved practice. This includes providing suitable instruction (for all pupils according to their needs) being sure that pupils know and understand fully what they are expected to do and are competent to do it. When the classroom becomes a science laboratory, with pupils watching demonstrations and engaging in practical work, good levels of supervision are crucial. Teachers need to monitor pupils' behaviour and be aware of different needs and changing circumstances
- Acting as a good role model for pupils. For example, by wearing safety goggles or rubber gloves when appropriate
- Providing curriculum opportunities that encourage pupils to take responsibility for their own safety and the safety of others. This will include issuing safety rules, explaining what they mean and why they are necessary and providing regular reminders
- Reporting all safety related incidents such as accidents or 'near misses' so that others can learn from them. The general school safety policy should have a procedure for recording such occurrences and any that relate specifically to science could be used to update the safety information included with point-of-use-texts as previously discussed
- Referring to appropriate safety guidance and model risk assessments such as that provided by LEAs, ASE and recommended texts such as *Be Safe!* when carrying out practical science activities with pupils.

Procedures

The policy should include details of the procedures that are in place to ensure that all involved in science teaching understand and fulfil their responsibilities such that the policy is implemented effectively. For example it should include details of:

- Induction procedures for staff (including new members of staff and trainee teachers) and details of on-going training in safety management relevant to science
- A statement about risk assessment and how it should be used when pupils are carrying out open-ended practical work and projects in science, including any special measures for fieldwork and off-site activities
- Procedures to be used when taking out, setting up and putting away apparatus used in science activities
- How pupils are to be trained in safety awareness. Specific codes of conduct during practical work
- What to do if pupils misbehave in practical science and endanger themselves or others
- Details of the action to be taken in the event of an accident or emergency. The whole school policy should have a general procedure in place for such occurrences. The science policy should refer to incidents that may occur during science lessons. For example, if a pupil gets a chemical in their eye, it should immediately be washed out with plenty of water and than medical advice sought
- A summary of dos and don'ts for all staff.

Regular checks

There is a statutory requirement for checking mains electrical equipment and safety equipment, such as fire extinguishers, and schools should have procedures in place to ensure that this occurs. Apart from mains electrical equipment there are few pieces of apparatus used in primary science that are likely to pose a risk. However, when an annual audit of science equipment is carried out it is worth checking that protective equipment such as safety goggles and rubber gloves are in good condition and that glass and plastic apparatus are not damaged, e.g. by being cracked, or having sharp edges.

Pupils

Devising codes of conduct for science is a useful way of alerting pupils to the potential risks involved in practical science and the safety policy should include copies of such codes. Appropriate codes can be formulated for each year group and can be used as part of the strategy to help develop pupils' safety awareness as they get older. The policy should emphasise the importance of teaching pupils actively about any safety rules and the reasons for them.

Safety resources

The policy should include a list of safety resources and details of how these can be accessed. These resources are best stored centrally and should include published reference materials to assist teaching, details of model risk assessments adopted by the employer, relevant publications and circulars produced by bodies such as the Health and Safety Executive, Child Accident Protection Trust, Local Education Authorities and the Department for Education and Employment.

Many of these procedures already take place in primary schools, but often informally. It is important that a policy is not only in place but that it is implemented and monitored. The guidelines suggested will help schools not only meet their legal and professional duties but also to develop a safety culture that controls and minimises the chance that pupils will be exposed to unacceptable risks during science activities.

It is important that class teachers, at the heart of the learning process, are not only aware of their responsibilities, but also feel confident and competent to fulfil them through their classroom practice. It is for the class teacher to employ a variety of teaching methods and strategies to create a safe learning environment for pupils. To ignore this is to deny responsibility and may even impact on the curriculum opportunities made available to pupils. It is the class teacher who has to ensure agreed procedures are implemented, that resources are appropriate and stored carefully, and that children are supervised when working with objects (particularly as they might be tempted to put them into their mouth, ear or nostrils). However, teachers also have the responsibility to teach pupils to recognise and control risks for themselves (as required by the National Curriculum for Science), consequently it is important that some of the science activities in which they participate involve an element of risk. The next section suggests an approach to planning learning experiences in science that are designed to promote the development of pupils' safety awareness.

Planning lessons to promote safety and learning about safety

Having recognised that safety issues should be considered when any practical science work is being planned, there are certain topics and methods that are particularly appropriate when the main learning objective is the raising of safety awareness. These include:

- heating and burning
- working with electricity
- using chemicals, simple tools and equipment
- any open-ended practical work
- investigations that pupils design themselves
- fieldwork using the outdoor classroom and any off-site visits.

A useful first step in deciding when it is sensible to focus on raising safety awareness is to carry out an audit of the school science curriculum with the aim of identifying topics that provide the best opportunities for this focus. A resource that could be used when carrying out such an audit is the exemplar *Scheme of Work for Science at Key Stages 1 and 2* (Qualifications and Curriculum Authority, 1998) that was sent to all maintained primary schools in England and Wales in July 1998. This divides the Key Stage 1 and 2 programmes of study into 37 units, each of which includes health and safety guidance designed to help teachers plan safe practical activities. It also contains guidance to show how attainment target 1 (Experimental and Investigative Science), and the requirements of the introductions to the Key Stage 1 and 2 programmes of study, can be integrated and taught in the context of the other sections of the programmes of study.

Having identified topics in the curriculum that could be used to help promote pupils' safety awareness, the next step could be to decide on how best to achieve continuity and progression in pupils' understanding of the attitudes and skills that are being addressed. In common with all other approaches to teaching and learning, it is important that planning takes account of children's perceptions and understanding of the topic being addressed. McWhirter (1997) discusses the relationship between children's cognitive and moral development and their understanding of safety related concepts. Her suggestions for developing the safety education curriculum in primary aged pupils are summarised in Figure 7.3. These provide a useful starting point when planning for continuity and progression in pupils' safety awareness. At Key Stage 1 the emphasis should be on helping pupils to understand that there are a variety of hazards and associated risks in many aspects of their lives and that following certain rules can minimise the chance of an accident happening. Whenever a practical science activity is being carried out simple 'rules for keeping safe' can be given to the pupils and illustrated with concrete examples of the possible consequences of not following the rules, e.g. they might cut themselves with scissors or burn themselves on something hot. The words used to explain the risks should be

FIG 7.3
A summary of
McWhirter's suggestions
for developing the safety
education curriculum
(Based on McWhirter,
1997)

Understanding pupils' stages of development and their understanding of safety related concepts.

Starting points

- 4–5-year-old children have little or no understanding of the word 'accident' or the concept of 'risk'.
- Understanding of the word 'accident' is reasonably well developed by the age of 7 or 8.
- 10-year-old children commonly equate risk with extreme danger or minor criminal activity.
- Most 11-year-olds understand the wider meanings associated with the term 'risk'.

The need to consider safety issues using a range of strategies and unfamiliar contexts

- Children under seven years old can learn from concrete examples and apply a learned response to an appropriate situation.
- Older children (seven and above) should be taught that a previously learned response is not always appropriate.
- Structured play can be used to help pupils decide on appropriate strategies and understand the potential consequences of their decisions.

The use of language to help develop pupils' understanding

- Words such as 'health', 'safety' and 'risk' are all abstract nouns and children require considerable linguistic ability to understand or convey their meaning.
- Phrases such as 'keeping safe' and 'being healthy' should be used when talking with children.
- The word 'risky' should be introduced with concrete examples such as, 'It is risky to run when you are carrying scissors, because you might fall and cut yourself.'
- It is important to avoid implying that objects have intentions by saying, for example, 'Come away from the fire, you will burn yourself', rather than, 'Come away from the fire, it will burn you.'

The shift of responsibility from the teacher to the pupil

- Around 50 per cent of 10-year-old children think that it is the responsibility of someone else to keep them safe.
- By the age of 11 years, 70 per cent of children recognise that they are also responsible for keeping themselves safe.
- Children may not show concern for the safety of others until they reach the age of 11.
- 9–10 years old pupils should be encouraged to recognise health and safety issues from the perspective of others using concrete examples from everyday life.

---

chosen carefully to ensure that pupils' understanding of the safety issues is not hampered by their linguistic abilities.

As the pupils get older, McWhirter suggests that the emphasis should be on shifting the responsibility for recognising hazards and controlling risks from the teacher to the pupil. Rather than giving pupils a set of rules, teachers can begin to help pupils judge for themselves what actions are appropriate to keep themselves and others safe and healthy. Clear safety rules will still be needed, particularly if the risks are great, but these rules can be formulated following a class discussion of risks. Doing this will help the pupils to understand the reasons for the rules and realise that they have a responsibility to keep themselves and others safe and healthy. Verbal reminders, posters around the classroom as well as the monitoring of pupils' actions will also contribute to a safety ethos.

Planning lessons that will raise safety awareness

> *Keeping safe is a practical skill and should be taught in an active way. Learning by your mistakes in the real world is risky, but teachers and health professionals can provide controlled, structured settings which challenge children's strategies for keeping safe and extend their knowledge and skills.*
>
> (McWhirter, 1997, p. 8)

Many aspects of safety awareness relating to different topics can be addressed using resources such as pictures, books, video and computer programmes (see Support material). However, most teachers would endorse McWhirter's claim that practical activities in science provide an ideal opportunity for pupils to gain first hand experience of some elements of controlled risk. Before carrying out such activities it is vital to conduct a risk assessment. Once it is decided that the risks involved in the activity are acceptable, then it can be carried out with pupils. At all times teachers must adopt procedures that are considered regular and approved, as these have reliably avoided foreseeable accidents without reducing the challenge and developmental value of science for pupils.

When the activity is carried out in a lesson the risks involved can be discussed with the pupils and their responses used to help them understand why, for safety reasons, it is important to follow a particular procedure and the measures that can be taken to control risk. Such discussions, 'ways to keep safe,' as part of a lesson will also help to develop pupils' life skills and understanding of risks in general. Pupils ideas can also be used each time a lesson focusing on safety awareness is taught. Discussions could focus on:

- Identifying the hazards
- Assessing the risks
- Controlling the risks
- Knowing what to do if an accident happens
- Devising a safe procedure for the activity
- Relating the activity to everyday contexts
- Developing self-responsibility.

Activity Observing a burning candle
Learning objectives To develop:

- Observational and descriptive skills by careful examination of a candle as it burns
- Safety awareness through the joint formulation of a safe procedure for the activity
- Knowledge and understanding of hazards associated with fire and action to be taken in case of fire or burns.

Safety focus	Questions to ask / examples to discuss / teaching points
Identifying the hazards	Have you ever burnt yourself? What did it feel like?
Risk assessment	How could this candle flame harm you? How could the flame start a bigger fire?
Risk control	What could you do to make sure that you don't burn yourself? What should we do to make sure that a fire doesn't start?
If an accident happens	What should you do if you did burn yourself? What should we do if a fire did start?
Safe procedure	Using the children's responses to questions like these, the teacher and pupils can together formulate a safe approach to the activity: ■ the candle should be placed inside a metal tray (e.g. a baking tray) and supported by a layer of sand – this helps to keep the candle stable and also serves to catch any hot wax that runs down the candle ■ long hair should be tied back ■ loose clothing should not be worn ■ pupils must not put anything into the flame or lean over it ■ the flame must be kept away from things that might easily catch fire such as paper or curtains ■ a bucket of sand should be kept in the classroom in case a small fire did start ■ pupils should be reminded about the fire drill evacuation procedure ■ burns should be treated immediately by putting the burnt area into cold water and leaving it there for at least 10 minutes.
Everyday contexts	Birthday cakes, candlelit dinners, use of candles during power cuts.
Developing self-responsibility	Importance of treating fire and hot things with respect and knowing what to do if an unwanted fire starts. Correct first aid procedure for burns or scalds.

FIG 7.4
Detailed planning notes for a risk assessment procedure at Key Stage 1

The potential value of this approach is illustrated in Figures 7.4 and 7.5. These provide detailed suggestions that could be used for developing pupils' safety awareness in the context of heating and burning at Key Stages 1 and 2. This topic has been selected because practical work in science, at levels

Activity Investigating the fire resistance of different fabrics

Learning objectives To develop:

- Procedural science skills by devising an investigation
- Safety awareness in the context of a potentially hazardous activity
- Knowledge and understanding of hazards associated with fire and action to be taken in case of fire or burns.

	Questions to ask / examples to discuss
Identifying the hazards	Questions to ask: Have you ever seen a house on fire? How could the fire have started? How could the fire have been prevented? How could we test fabrics to see how fire resistant they are? What could we use to set fire to them? How can we do this safely?
Risk assessment	What are the dangers involved in carrying out this investigation?
Risk control	What could you do to make sure that you don't burn yourself? How should you use matches? What size piece of fabric should we use? What should we do to make sure that a fire doesn't start in the classroom?
If an accident happens	What should you do if you did burn yourself? What should we do if a fire did start?
Safe procedure	Using the children's responses to questions like these, the teacher and pupils can together formulate a safe approach to the activity. The procedures listed in the previous example will all apply. In addition: ■ the teacher could demonstrate the safe procedure for lighting matches and then allow pupils to light their own candles ■ the pupils should be standing and not sitting when carrying out this activity so that they can quickly move out of the way if an accident does occur ■ small pieces of fabric should be used ■ eye protection (safety goggles/glasses) should be worn ■ the classroom should be adequately ventilated to prevent build up of smoke or fumes ■ a safe procedure for disposing of test fabrics and spent matches should be used.
Everyday contexts	Lighting fires, using fire guards, the use of fire resistant fabrics for clothing and furniture, the dangers of careless disposal of cigarettes, the dangers of smoke in domestic fires, the value of smoke alarms, firework safety, treating burns.
Developing self-responsibility	Treating fire with respect. Knowing what to do if an unwanted fire starts. Importance of fire drills. Dangers of lighting fires outside in hot dry weather. Careful disposal of spent matches, cigarettes and glass jars and bottles.

FIG 7.5
Detailed planning notes for a risk assessment at Key Stage 2

ranging from early explorations in infant schools up to advanced level research work in universities, often involves heating things. All primary-aged children will have had some everyday experiences connected with heating and burning, e.g. for cooking, making hot drinks and heating homes. Fire has a fascination for children, they want to light the birthday cake candles, twigs in barbecues and to hold sparklers. Many children will have experienced the pain of being burnt or scalded but although these are powerful learning experiences they are best avoided in the classroom!

The Key Stage 1 activity 'Observing a burning candle', outlined in Figure 7.4, could be used in a sequence of lessons for unit 1D, 'Light and dark', of the QCA exemplar scheme of work. Among the anticipated learning outcomes listed for this unit are that children should:
■ Make comparisons between light sources in terms of brightness or colour
■ Recognise that lights, e.g. bonfires, fireworks, candles, show up best when it is dark and that they can see these because they are light sources.

The guidance on safety reads: 'Night lights and stubby candles are almost impossible to knock over. All naked flames are best used in a metal tray, e.g. baking tray filled with dry sand. Children should be kept away from flames.' This safety guidance constitutes regular and approved practice and must be followed if this activity is carried out with pupils.

The suggested Key Stage 2 activity 'Investigating the fire resistance of different fabrics' outlined in Figure 7.5 could be part of a lesson sequence for unit 6D, 'Reversible and irreversible changes', of the QCA scheme. Among the learning outcomes given for this unit are that children should be able to:
■ Describe what is seen when common materials, e.g. wax, wood, natural gas are burned
■ Recognise that in each case new materials are made, e.g. ash, gases that cannot be seen
■ Classify burning as an irreversible change
■ Identify hazards associated with burning materials.

The safety guidance which should be followed reinforces and develops Key Stage 1 guidance: 'Burn materials using a small candle or night light standing in a metal tray, e.g. a baking tray containing dry sand. Do not use more than a piece the size of a small postage stamp because plastics and synthetic fabrics often give off poisonous gases when they are burned. Avoid the use of PVC. Any LEA/school guidelines must be observed'.

Conclusions

As discussed in Chapter 1, teachers could eliminate all aspects of risk from the learning experiences they plan and this may help to ensure that while pupils are in their care they do not come to any harm. But accidents will and still do happen. The duty of the teacher is to demonstrate that reasonable care had been provided. However, the teacher's duty of care goes beyond the immediate concerns of the activity taking place. There is also a duty to prepare pupils for life outside the classroom and the central role of safety education should be to help pupils learn how to become responsible, safety aware, members of society. This chapter sets out an approach to the management and teaching of primary science that illustrates that it is possible for teachers to plan motivating lessons that involve some degree of risk and, at the same time, to follow regular and approved practice. The safest people are those who have been taught how to handle potentially dangerous situations properly, rather than those who have never been exposed to them. Practical activities in primary science provide an ideal context for raising pupils' safety awareness through exposing them to risks in a controlled setting.

References

ASE (Association for Science Education) (1990) *Be Safe! Some Aspects of Safety in School Science and Technology for Key Stages 1 and 2*, 2nd edn., Hatfield: Association for Science Education.

ASE (Association for Science Education) (1995) *Be Safe! Some Aspects of Health and Safety in the Scottish Curriculum Environmental Studies 5–14*, Hatfield: Association for Science Education.

Borrows, P. (1993) 'Safety in secondary school science' in Hull, R. (ed.) *ASE Secondary Teachers' Handbook*, Hemel Hempstead: Simon and Schuster Education.

Borrows, P. (1997) 'Safe as houses or as safe as the primary classroom?' *Primary Science Review*, **47**: pp. 12–13.

Department of Education and Science (1990) *Animals and Plants in Schools: Legal Aspects (Administrative Memorandum 3/90)*, London: Department of Education and Science.

DFE (1993) Initial Teacher Training, Primary Phase (Circular 14/93), London: HMSO.

DFE (1995) *Science in the National Curriculum*, London: HMSO.

DfEE (1998) *Teaching: High Status, High Standards (Circular 4/98)*, London: Department for Education and Employment.

McWhirter, J. (1997) *Spiralling into Control? A Review of the Development of Children's Understanding of Safety Related Concepts.* Paper submitted to the Royal Society for the Prevention of Accidents, Birmingham.

Qualifications and Curriculum Authority (1998) *A Scheme of Work for Key Stages 1 and 2: Science*, London: Qualifications and Curriculum Authority.

Raper, G. and Stringer, J. (1987) *Encouraging Primary Science*, London: Cassell.

Tawney, D. (1992) 'Assessment of risk and school science', *School Science Review*, **74** (267): 7–14.

Vincent, R. and Borrows, P. (1992) 'Science department safety policies', *School Science Review*, **73** (254): 9–13.

Support material

The Association for Science Education (ASE) have produced an INSET package *Safety in Science for Primary Schools* that supports their *Be Safe!* booklet. *The Teacher's Book* supporting the *ASE Science and Technology in Society (SATIS)* 8–14 materials produced by the ASE (1992) offers many useful ideas for raising safety awareness as does the *Science and Technology for the under 8s* material (ASE, 1996). The ASE journals (*Primary Science Review* and *Education in Science*) regularly include advice and information regarding health and safety issues.

The Child Accident Prevention Trust (CAPT) have published *The Risk Pack – A teacher's resource to help children assess and manage risk*. This is intended as a 'tool kit' for teachers and contains many suggestions to help teachers tackle the subject in various ways, from a topic base or subject specialist point of view.

The Royal Society for the Prevention of Accidents (RoSPA) produce many teaching resources that can be used in the context of primary science. For example, the 'Go Again with Science' series of booklets includes suggestions for practical classroom activities designed to link science with the development of road safety awareness. Many pictorial resources are suitable for younger children and their journal *Safety Education* regularly includes suggestions for helping raise pupils' safety awareness.

The Institute of Chemical Engineers (IChemE) have recently produced a 'Health and Safety Activities Box'. This includes over 100 activities designed by primary science advisers from the Northamptonshire Inspection and

Advisory Service in collaboration with the Health and Safterty Commission and Executive.

Other support materials are available from Local Education Authorities (these organisations often run INSET courses concerned with safety in primary science), the Consortium of Local Education Authorities for the Provision of School Science (CLEAPSS) Service and the Scottish Schools Equipment Research Centre (SSERC).

Many books about primary science provide general advice concerning safety issues but relatively few include specific advice for raising pupils' safety awareness. Two exceptions are *Opportunities for Science in the Primary School* (Peacock, A., Trentham Books, Stoke-on-Trent, 1997) and *Children and Primary Science* (Jarvis, T., Cassell, London, 1991) both include a number of useful practical suggestions.

Acknowledgments

My thanks go to the primary science coordinators and Exeter University trainee teachers with whom I have discussed these issues and who gave me useful feedback on the suggested approach for planning with safety in mind. Thanks also to Martin Gomberg (Education Officer for the Royal Society for the Prevention of Accidents) for a copy of the paper by McWhirter.

Chapter 8

Safe practice in the 'outdoor classroom'

Sue Thomas

Within the last decade educational initiatives such as the National Curriculum have, in part, been instrumental in widening the boundaries of the classroom, the concept of educational knowledge and how this is transmitted. Many young people are now involved in a wider range of curriculum activities and the setting in which learning takes place has also diversified.

On almost every day of the school year, parties of school children are engaged in a range of educational activities, some of which can only be offered and experienced outside the school environment and in the 'outdoor classroom'. Visits to urban and countryside venues, historical sites, beach and coastal environments and working farms are becoming a regular feature of modern day education. However, while it could be argued that young people now have increased opportunities to learn away from the school and in, about and through the outdoor environment, this potential expansion is not unproblematic. Unfortunately, the educational benefits of the off-site and outdoor classroom have been overshadowed by a number of well-publicised accidents involving school children. As identified in Chapter 1, there is also a prevailing social trend, not only towards making things safer, but also towards seeking compensation for acts or omissions that result in personal injury. The concern for the safety and well-being of children is, therefore, part of a much broader cultural phenomenon which is beginning to affect the everyday lives and working practices of teachers in schools.

This chapter focuses on safe practice in relation to educational activities and experiences that take pupils away from the school and into the outdoor classroom. Here, the complex interplay of human and environmental factors is a significant issue and one which differentiates the learning context from that found on the school site and within the classroom. Drawing on case studies and research on accidents in the outdoors, this chapter begins by considering the unique nature of the outdoor classroom and what can be learned from tragedy in terms of understanding accidents in the outdoors. It also identifies supervision as the basic principle of safe practice and discusses elements of this and the implications for teachers' practice and pupils' safety across a range of outdoor activities and settings.

The nature of the outdoor classroom

The nature of the outdoor classroom is becoming increasingly varied, involving a variety of environments, activities and seasons. Although it is well recognised that the various forms of out-of-school activities can make a valuable contribution to the development of young people, in terms of helping to increase investigative skills, taking on new responsibilities, developing greater independence and experiencing new personal, social and educational challenges, there is also a common perception that such activities are inherently hazardous. While it is true that some curriculum activities, more than others, offer the potential for accident and hazard many (Purves, 1997; Bonnington, 1997) would argue that there is risk in almost everything that we do and that for some activities, it is the risk itself which provides the challenge. However, safety can never be guaranteed or ensured because chance, unforeseen conditions, improper decisions and judgment can all interact to generate hazard and risk. Despite appropriate management, organisation and close supervision of pupils, schools like other social environments are susceptible to accident or risk. No amount of planning can guarantee that a visit or trip will be totally incident free.

It goes without saying that educational activities, whether taking place on or off the school site, should never be dangerous. However, outdoor locations and activities away from the school are often selected for their unfamiliarity, new and stimulating opportunities that can often create adventure, challenge, uncertainty, excitement and, additional risk. Working in the outdoor classroom demands of teachers additional skills, competencies and judgment. For instance, some activities by virtue of their remote location will require a level of self-sufficiency, organisation and management that is quite different from that required in the classroom or in more public areas. Pedagogy and practice in the outdoor classroom is often very different. Experiential and experience-based styles of learning, that are prevalent in the medium of the outdoors, require teachers to be able to manage the learning environment often without being fully in control of the learning process. Pupils are often given a greater scope and responsibility for their own learning. On occasions this may mean that pupils work independently of the teacher, are not always working within sight and that supervisory styles are more flexible. Apart from a total familiarity with the activity and working environment, an increased level of planning and preparation, the outdoor teacher will need good judgment. As a key aspect in the decision-making process, it is perhaps the most important constituent of all outdoor leadership. Good judgment is often regarded as the buffer between education and mis-education and adventure and mis-adventure.

LEAs, in their guidance to schools relating to educational visits, increasingly recognise that it is not just the so called 'hazardous' and adventurous activities, such as climbing, canoeing or mountain walking (where the inclusion of risk may be an essential and desirable element of the learning process) that are susceptible to accidents. Everyday situations such as those involving transportation, road traffic or proximity to water have potential for accidents to occur. In this respect, the nature of the activity should not necessarily imply that there is any greater or lesser degree of real risk. Research evidence (Brackenreg, 1997) suggests that the common perception of adventurous outdoor activities being inherently risky is not supported by the accident data. Compared with competitive sports and the occupational workplace, the reported injury rates were low. Similarly, Jacobs (1996) reported that more children are killed or injured travelling to and from outdoor activity centres than at the centres themselves. A survey by the Outward Bound Trust (reported in Hansard) similarly found that more children were hurt falling down stairs at activity centres than injured while participating in the adventure activities themselves. These findings would tend to suggest that some outdoor and adventurous activities are less risky than some aspects of everyday living and other types of educational visits.

Although the Altwood inquiry into the deaths of four boys, who fell while on a school outing to Austria, concluded that teachers working in the outdoors are entitled to an expectation of obedience to rules, self-discipline, common sense and responsible behaviour (related to their age and ability), away from the restrictions of the classroom and in stimulating and adventurous environments, the behaviour of normally conforming pupils cannot be taken for granted (see 'close calls – Marloes again' *JAEOL* 11 (1), 1994, pp. 4–5). Providing a standard of care in the outdoor classroom means recognising that, by virtue of their limited life experience, pupils' perception of risk is likely to be limited. This along with an inquisitive nature and natural curiosity can be a recipe for tragedy. Additional strategies to ensure that pupils have minimal opportunity to move beyond the specified boundaries of safety are, therefore, required.

Finally, analysing the anatomy of accidents in the outdoors reveals that certain combinations of environmental factors can lead to dynamic circumstances (see Hale, 1983; Priest, 1996; Thomas and Raymond, 1996). Factors such as the weather, environmental vagaries and seasonal variations are significant considerations for those who work in the outdoor classroom because they create dynamic and sometimes unpredictable hazards for the unwary. Many incidents affecting pupils have occurred by or in the sea and open water environments are particularly susceptible in this respect and are, therefore, potentially very hazardous. It is the presence of the environmental factors that makes the outdoor context such a different one from that found in the classroom and, as will be seen later in this chapter, an understanding of the interrelationship between environmental and human hazards is an important element of managing safe practice in the outdoor classroom.

Managing safe practice

Working within their legal, professional and moral duty to ensure a safe outdoor learning environment requires the teacher to identify, manage and control any risks to health and well-being. However, safe practice in the outdoor classroom is just as dependent on safety education, the creation of a safety ethos and the application of basic principles, as it is upon regulation and legislation.

The creation of a safety culture involves educating all those involved about how and why accidents happen. The ability to assess the risks and dangers of everyday activities and to be able to act accordingly is an essential life skill. The National Curriculum now specifically acknowledges that these skills are essential for pupils and this is explicit in subjects such as science, design and technology and physical education. Similarly, Circular 4/98, which outlines the requirements for courses of initial teacher training, specifies that those to be awarded qualified teacher status should have a working knowledge and understanding of health and safety legislation and common law duty to ensure that pupils are healthy and safe on educational visits, school outings or field trips. The OFSTED guidance on the inspection of schools also requires inspectors to assess whether the school is successful in promoting the health, safety and general well-being of its pupils and has a responsible attitude towards the education and training of pupils in safe practice (DfEE, 1995, p. 91). For teachers and pupils working in the outdoor classroom this means understanding the outdoor environment, learning from tragedy and the experiences of others.

This said, opportunities to learn from the experiences of others are often limited. Within the UK we do not currently have an off-site activities accident database on which we can draw to provide information and an indication of which activities might produce more than their fair share of accidents. Furthermore, with the exception of major accidents involving school children, most do not reach the public domain and the fact that the majority of litigation cases are settled out of court means that little is ever heard of them. Research (Raymond and Thomas, forthcoming) shows that although teachers are aware of accidents involving immediate colleagues, understanding remains at superficial and anecdotal levels. This does not always help teachers to learn from real events or modify their practice. The outdoor adventure profession has recognised the learning potential of accidents, both major and minor, and has attempted to address this through the sharing and evaluation of 'close call' and 'near miss' incidents. These are defined as incidents where no harm results, but where there was potential for serious injury. It is this sort of open and reflective approach to incidents and potential accidents that will help increase knowledge and understanding and play a significant role in the creation of a safety culture.

Understanding why accidents happen

An analysis of four school trips into the outdoor classroom, undertaken by Thomas (1994) and Raymond and Thomas (1996), identified that there are similarities as to why accidents happen. Using a case study approach and documentary analysis, data collected on the Cairngorm Tragedy, 1971; Stoke Poges Middle School's visit to Lands End, 1985; the Altwood School Easter Trip to Austria, 1988, and the Lyme Bay Tragedy, 1993, show that accidents occurred because of a combination of factors emerging from both the environmental and human domains. These related to some or all of the following points:

■ poor decision-making, judgment and subsequent reaction to the situation/incident
■ lack of adequate and appropriate supervision, group management and organisation
■ over-estimation of:
  (a) the teachers/leaders ability – knowledge, understanding and competence;
  (b) the pupils' sense of responsibility
■ under-estimation of potential hazard and risk.

The analysis of what happened and why, highlighted the importance of understanding the presence of different types of dangers and raises a number of issues relating to the principles of safe practice. The analysis also supported Hale's (1983) view that most accidents out of doors occur when two types of dangers (human and environmental) are present *and* combine at the same time (Hale, 1983; Priest, 1996). For example, in the Lyme Bay accident, the cold and wet conditions along with the sea state, wind direction and strength created five environmental hazards. In addition, the inadequate equipment, pupil and leader inexperience, fatigue and poor judgment created five human hazards. The likelihood of an accident often depends upon the number of hazards and their interaction. The greater the hazards, the more likely it is that there will be an accident because more combinations among the environmental and human dangers are possible. Unfortunately, in the Lyme Bay accident the interaction and combination of five environmental and five human dangers, created a situation in which an accident was 25 times more likely than had there been just one danger in the environmental and human domains.

Similarly, with the Land's End tragedy in 1985, when four middle school children drowned, the combination of pupil curiosity, pupil and teacher limited perception of hazard, the accessibility of the sea and the prevailing sea state (swell) created conditions whereby an increased level of risk was present. Hale's approach is helpful to all teachers using the outdoor classroom because an identification and assessment of both the environmental and human hazards can enable the teacher to recognise and determine the potential level of risk. It also makes the point that in relation to managing safe practice out of doors, teachers ignore the human dimension at their peril. It is often the participatory behaviour, attitudes and actions of the participants, rather than the activity itself, that generates risk. As Ford and Blanchard (1985) conclude, 'it is people who cause accidents, people in the wrong place at wrong times with wrong equipment making wrong decisions' (p. 150).

Basic principles of safe practice

Knowledge of how and why accidents happen can, therefore, raise generic principles related to safe practice in the outdoors and provides an effective basis for modifications to practice that should minimise the occurrence of injury. Similarly, understanding the factors contributing to accidents allows them to be foreseen and anticipated, so that the focus is proactive and preventative rather than reactive.

Evidence from accident research in the outdoors (Thomas, 1994; Raymond & Thomas, 1996; Brackenreg, 1997) clearly points to supervision as being the major factor in low injury rates and safe participation. This finding is also supported by Van de Smissen, (1990) who reports that 80 per cent of injury claims involving recreation, physical education and outdoor sports contain supervision issues. In the UK, case law has also identified supervision as being crucial to fulfilling the duty of care required by Health and Safety legislation. As well as being a basic principle of safe practice, reasonable supervision is also the first line of defence against charges of legal liability and negligence. Supervision issues relating to the organisation of day-to-day procedures and arrangements for, and the conduct of, visits, are also elements of an OFSTED inspection. Evaluating and reporting on the extent to which a school is successful in promoting the health, safety and general well-being of its pupils is an essential aspect of the inspection process (DfEE, 1995, p. 91).

Supervising outdoor activities

As outlined by Raymond in Chapter 1, the law requires that teachers provide a standard of care that 'from an objective point of view can be reasonably expected from teachers generally applying skill and awareness of children's problems, needs and susceptibilities' (NUT, 1995, p. 4). This is the common law principle of being *in loco parentis*. In practice, this means that a teacher must ensure supervision of the pupils and activity or visit as professional standards and common sense demand. What is reasonable supervision, when must supervision be provided and how much supervision is enough, are key considerations and judgments in managing safe practice in the outdoor classroom. However, these are difficult questions to answer because there are not always established standards and it is difficult to frame statements to cover all eventualities. This said, court rulings have shown that activities that carry a greater inherent risk must be carried out with this in mind and that in reality, the level of care expected of teachers may be higher than, for example, a parent because more is expected of a trained professional (BAALPE, 1995, p. 22; Devon LEA, 1996, p. 21; Leeds LEA, 1997, p. 1).

As suggested, one of the most frequent accusations of breach of duty is lack of adequate supervision (De Haven, 1994), so it is important that teachers are clear about how supervision is defined and the implications for their practice. Supervision involves more than just being there as a presence to oversee and protect pupils from dangerous conditions, activities and environments. As Kaiser (1986) has suggested, it also encompasses, 'the preparation, planning and maintenance necessary to allow the activity to proceed safely' (p. 29).

Principles of supervision in the outdoor classroom

Experience in the management and organisation of school trips, along with case study analysis of some accidents to pupils while in the outdoor classroom (Thomas, 1994), suggests that it is important to consider general supervisory issues as well as those in relation to specific elements of the trip or activity. Although there are areas of overlap, supervisory considerations should relate to the following:

- General supervisory considerations
- Issues related to personnel
- Planning the activity
- Safe conduct of the activity.

General supervisory considerations

The minimum level of supervision required for activities is often determined by LEA guidance or regulations concerning recommended staffing ratios and leadership qualifications. Teachers should work within these. Additionally, for most outdoor pursuit activities the National Governing Body also provides guidance on staffing ratios and recommended teacher/leader qualifications.

While the level and type of supervision depends on a number of factors such as the age, aptitude and experience of the children, the skill and experience of the staff, the nature and length of the activity or trip, the location of the activity and availability of assistance, there are certain principles to be observed in the management of safe practice in the off-site and outdoor classroom. The very nature of off-site activities makes it desirable to have at least two or more accompanying teachers. There is always the possibility that a problem may arise; a search may need to be made for a separated pupil, a pupil may need to be taken to hospital, back to school, etc. A second teacher would provide greater options in terms of decision-making and continuity of supervision. Additionally, teachers driving minibuses should not normally be responsible for pupil supervision during the journey, although this will depend on factors such as the age of the pupils and the length of the journey.

However, all off-site activities are demanding for teachers and the longer an activity lasts, the more important it is to provide adequate staffing. This is particularly so if the trip occurs towards the end of the school day and extends into the evening. Teachers are less likely to supervise efficiently and vigilantly if they are over tired and provision should be made for breaks and relaxation. Recognising this, and the high level of accidents related to the use of minibuses and cars, many LEAs recommend that on long journeys, teacher-drivers should operate within the Department of the Environment, Transport and the Regions (DETR), *Drivers' Hours: Rules for Road Passenger Vehicles: PSV 375 regulations.* These state that, 'after 4.5 hours of cumulative or continuous driving, a driver must take a break of at least 45 minutes (or two or three breaks of no less than 15 minutes' duration during or after the driving period so that the total break adds up to at least 45 minutes in the 4.5 hours of driving)' (p. 5). The maximum period of driving to be undertaken in one day is nine hours, after which a period of rest of at least 11 consecutive hours should be taken. On long journeys, the use of two drivers should be considered (see also Devon LEA, 1994, p. 19). This is because the length of driving time should also be considered in relation to the time already spent teaching and involved in other aspects of professional work during the day. Similarly, length of driving time and the number of rest breaks should be adjusted if abnormal or difficult driving conditions are encountered (e.g. continental driving, bad weather/night driving). In this sense, judgments about the level of staffing and supervision need to take into consideration a number of factors – not just the recommended ratios and regulations.

Analysis of school tragedies also highlights a number of principles relating to the level of supervision and monitoring of pupils:

- Care should always be taken to ensure that if the party is divided for any reason the recommended staffing ratio should be maintained when supervising the different groups
- Frequent headcounts were also recommended to be a key factor in the supervision of parties and when visiting busy public places. Distinguishing, easily recognisable and common clothing such as school uniform, hats or badges can assist this procedure. However, DfEE (1998) guidance suggests that pupils should not display their name clearly on their clothing, as this could result in them being isolated from the group by an apparently friendly and personal call
- A list of pupils on the trip should be carried by all supervising adults and if the party is divided into smaller groups, each group leader should have a list of those pupils under their charge
- In terms of the management and control of a party, small groups under the control of an individual supervisor can provide more effective supervision than a large party under the collective care of one or a number of teachers. This is particularly so when pupils are moving in busy places and where transportation is shared with members of the

public such as on ski lifts or the London Underground where keeping the party together can be difficult or induce unnecessary pressure.

A further basic principle, in relation to the level of supervision, is that when pupils with an identified special need participate, this should be reflected in a more generous staffing ratio. This will help maintain the safety of everyone on the visit, allow the special needs to be met and the pupil(s) the opportunity to participate fully. All accompanying adults should also be aware of which pupils have special needs and know the relevant procedures. It is well worth remembering that reasonable levels of supervision means meeting the needs of individual pupils, not just those of the average participant and that additional safety measures may need to be addressed at the planning stage.

The type of supervision (close, general, remote), is also an important consideration and this may vary according to the aims and objectives of the activity, experience of participants, risk to health and well-being, environment, etc. Close supervision (close enough to intervene if required) should occur when there is some risk of injury and when instruction is being provided. Less experienced pupils will also require closer supervision as they gain knowledge and competence. Those with less experience are most likely to be injured because they are often unaware of the potential hazards to themselves or others and may not recognise their own limitations. This said, it should be recognised that pupils familiar with the activity or environment can sometimes become over confident and attempt things beyond their ability. Supervisors need to anticipate this possibility and consider a controlling strategy. Similarly, pupils who may behave in ways that may endanger themselves or others should be closely supervised. This may mean that additional accompanying staff are required. The nature of some outdoor activities, such as field trips when pupils are collecting data, etc., may mean that pupils are working within sight of the teacher, but not under close supervision. General supervision, the kind commonly practised in the school playground, may be appropriate if dangerous conditions or behaviour are not immediately foreseeable. However, safe general supervision requires enough teachers to view and manage the whole working area. A principle of general supervision is that intervention is possible if needed.

Some activities such as scavenger hunts, environmental surveys or orienteering in the local park may require pupils to be self reliant, unaccompanied and out of sight of the teacher. In these circumstances the teacher will still remain responsible for the group, but will be providing remote supervision. Great care is needed in the planning, pupil preparation and practice of such activities. LEA guidance is that pupils should always work in pairs or small groups – never alone and the possibility of attacks on pupils should be considered when deciding on venue, level of supervision, etc. The safety of pupils working independently can be greatly enhanced by a gradual and progressive withdrawal of direct supervision using such strategies as shadowing pupils, spot checking at various times and venues and contact at pre-arranged locations/times. It is also important that pupils fully understand the aims and objectives of the independent work, are aware of the working boundaries (time, space and behavioural) and know the emergency procedures – should they get lost or injured.

Issues related to personnel

Competence, experience and the leadership qualities of judgment, anticipation and management are paramount in helping teachers to generate safe practice in the outdoor classroom. Hazards and risks may not be immediately apparent to those who are unfamiliar with the activity or location and despite good planning, safety of the group can often depend upon the on-the-spot interpretation of events, decisions and responses of those in charge. Teachers leading outdoor learning activities should, therefore, be skilled and experienced enough to modify their plans to meet any changed conditions and circumstances. Teachers with experience of the specific activity and location are better able to accurately anticipate the hazards, assess and judge the risks.

The judicious matching of leaders and supervisors with any special responsibilities and emergency procedures can also enhance safety. If prior consideration is given to the strengths and weaknesses of the accompanying adults, supervising staff can be used to their maximum efficiency. For instance, if an accompanying teacher on a coastal field trip is a non or weak swimmer, they should not be given responsibility for water safety. At least one of the teachers should have knowledge of and responsibility for first aid and carry a first aid kit. Contingency/emergency equipment appropriate for the location, such as spare clothing (warm/waterproof), a hot drink, mobile phone, etc., should also be carried.

Following a number of accidents to pupils in the outdoor environment, guidance, recommended practice and in the case of the Activity Centres (Young Person's Act) 1995 legislation, has established that appropriate experience and proven competence of the leaders is a key factor in the provision of reasonable supervision. It is also important that continuing professional development occurs, especially with activities where there is potential for risk, because the law expects those in charge of young people to be familiar with 'regular and approved practice' and able to use this in the planning and safe delivery of learning activities.

While responsibility for safety when working off-site lies predominantly in the hands of the teacher/leaders, pupils can and should also play their part. However, the nature of the activity and variables such as age, maturity, levels of understanding and prior experience can affect the degree to which it is reasonable to expect pupils to take some responsibility for safety. Additionally, pupils are only likely to take some responsibility for their own safety, and that of others, if they recognise that a safety culture exists and they have been taught about aspects of safe practice. Establishing a safety ethos for a trip means that pupils should be aware of the potential hazards and clearly understand their responsibility to follow any rules or procedures that have been implemented for their protection. Providing such information and guidance to pupils is an important part of pre-trip preparation and could include a discussion to identify the hazards and the drawing up of an agreed set of safety rules, to which the pupils agree to abide by (see Raymond and Thomas, forthcoming). Pupils also need to know what to do in an emergency situation and have the resources and skills to be able to act accordingly. For example, if pupils are orienteering in pairs or small groups, they need to know what to do if they get lost and have the equipment (whistle, compass, map) and ability to enable them to follow the established emergency procedure. At busy public venues such as theme parks, museums or historic attractions, all pupils should know what to do if approached by a stranger and where to go should they become separated from the group. In situations where they are working independently of the teacher, an emergency card with guidance and information on what to do should be carried by each child. Before embarking on the trip or activity, the leader should be satisfied that the pupils understand key safety information and are capable of undertaking the proposed activities.

Many activities and trips such as visits to working farms, activity centres, leisure centres, etc., involve the use of facilities and staff managed outside the control of Local Education Authorities. This involvement of outside agencies raises a number of important issues related to safety. The first concerns the responsibility of schools to use only those outside agencies that conform to the safety standards acceptable to the LEA. Or, where a licensing scheme is in place and the activities to be undertaken are licensable (such as with some adventure activities and commercial providers) that they are in fact licensed. Most LEAs provide guidance on the procedures to be followed to ensure, as far as is possible, the safety of pupils using outside agencies.

■ It is important to check the licence status of an external provider. Holding an Adventure Activities Licence is activity specific and means that a provider has been inspected and that the Licensing Authority is satisfied that appropriate safety measures are in place. Activity elements covered by the licence should be confirmed.
Other elements of the provision such as accommodation and catering arrangements are not covered by the licensing scheme and should be checked independently. In particular, accommodation security arrangements, recreational facilities for the group and provision for sick pupils or those with special needs should be considered.
A pre-visit inspection and/or a reference from previous users may help schools make sound judgments about the quality of provision offered.

■ At both the planning and delivery phases of the activity/trip the school and outside agency should negotiate and agree a programme appropriate for the age, abilities and needs of the pupils.

■ Finally, when responsibility for pupil safety is divided between the school and the outside agency, this responsibility must be clearly defined, clearly transferred and all those involved should know who is responsible, when and the extent of the responsibility.

Planning the activity

Thorough planning and preparation is recognised in the OFSTED framework as being an important prerequisite for good teaching and it is also a basic principle of safe practice. It involves a number of procedures so should take place as early as possible to ensure that all these are completed in good time. Planning for safety is considerably enhanced and focused if the activity has a clearly identified educational purpose. This should always be communicated to all involved and be closely matched to the age, ability and prior experience of the group. As identified earlier in this chapter, pupils will also need to be adequately prepared to meet the activity objectives and learning tasks. This would include educating pupils about safe working practices related to the activity/trip planned and should include topics such as basic safety related to transport, what to do if they become lost or separated from the main party, adequate clothing/footwear and safety rules for the trip.

Perhaps the most essential procedure in planning and preparation for off-site activities involves the teacher in risk management. As Whitlam has identified in Chapter 3, the first step in this process is risk assessment and the second step is to develop controlling strategies to minimise the possibility of accidents. Risk assessment is the process by which significant hazards present in an activity are identified and an estimation made of the extent of the risks involved. This should take into account any safety precautions and existing control measures already being taken. In the outdoor classroom context, this will require a consideration and assessment of the capabilities and limitations of the participants (pupils and leaders), any equipment being used, the environment in which the activity takes place, the hazards inherent in the activity and the supervisory and pedagogical styles employed. Hazard identification should focus on significant hazards that could forseeably pose a risk to health and well-being. In the outdoor context, Bailie (1996) has identified three main things that will cause death or disablement:

■ drowning (water, silage, slurry)
■ impact with something solid (e.g. falling from a height to the ground or being knocked over by a vehicle)
■ exposure/hypothermia.

The assessment of risks in the outdoor classroom should, therefore, focus on these main hazards and a consideration of how the interrelationship between the human and environmental factors might increase the likelihood of risk to health and safety.

Outdoor and environmental vagaries, seasonal and temporal variations all create different situations which means that each outdoor trip/activity must be assessed on its own merits. In this sense, it is important that every effort is made by leaders to familiarise themselves with the area to be visited. A pre-visit is recommended so that anticipation of the hazards, both human and environmental, can occur. Depending on the activity, it may also be prudent to seek guidance from local people, Tourist Boards or services. For instance, some remote 'honey pot' sites and car parks are renowned for attracting theft and vandalism. Heavy rain can make some routes impassable, tracks and paths slippery and so increase the risks. Local conditions can often create hazards and dangers that may not be readily apparent to those without such knowledge.

While familiarisation with the area to be visited is important, an essential part of the risk assessment procedure, that is often overlooked, is familiarisation with the mode of transport to be used. If this is a self-drive minibus, prior to the journey, a check should be carried out on basic safety features such as tyres, lights, windscreen washers/wipers, brakes, availability of first aid kit and fire extinguisher, fluid levels, doors (operate freely and close securely) and warning instruments. Driver effectiveness and fatigue is also influenced by poor driving position and conditions so, before setting off the driver should adjust the seat, the mirrors and check that they can reach all the essential controls.

Finally, an essential aspect of any off-site planning and preparation is to establish procedures to adopt in the case of an emergency. This could be an injury to a pupil, an illness requiring immediate medical treatment or a fatality. It could also mean missing children or involvement in a traffic accident. Figure 8.1 provides an example of recommended procedure to be followed by leaders and accompanying teachers in the event of an emergency incident. However, not all procedures will apply to all incidents.

If these arrangements are defined and clear to all, it will facilitate the efficiency with which they can be implemented and the emergency situation dealt with and resolved. Most LEAs in their guidance and regulations for out-of-school activities and visits have included such advice to party leaders and this should always be carried so that teachers immediately have the

---

- Ascertain the nature and extent of the emergency
- Render first aid and attend to any casualties
- Secure and protect the rest of the group from injury or danger and the attention of any press and media. Check all are accounted for, comforted and looked after
- Telephone the emergency services and/or Police as appropriate (the Police will alert specialist services such as Coastguards, Cliff Rescue, Air/Sea Rescue, Mountain Rescue)
- Arrange for the rest of the group to return to school/base (camp site, hostel, etc.), leaving at least one teacher at the incident site to liaise with the emergency services/assist with any search and accompany any casualties to hospital
- Telephone the contact/designated member of staff at school – give details of the incident (location, time, names of those involved), state the *nature* of the incident, the *level* of action required and *priority*. State the action taken so far
- Give your location and contact number
- Write down all relevant details while they are fresh in your mind. Photographs and diagrams may be useful. Preserve any vital evidence – if equipment is involved, keep this in its original condition
- Record any names and addresses of witnesses
- Restrict pupil access to telephones until the head teacher/contact person has had time to contact all those directly involved (parents/carers, etc.)
- Do not make any statements to the media, refer these to the school contact person/press officer/LEA press officer
- Do not discuss or admit legal liability
- Complete all accident forms and contact insurers

All those involved in the trip, including supervising teachers and other adults, pupils and their parents, should know:
- who will take charge in an emergency
- the arrangements for back up cover
- what they are expected to do in an emergency.

FIG 8.1
Recommended procedure in the event of an emergency

means of implementing them. During the tense and stressed moments of an emergency situation, they will also guide the teacher towards the appropriate, logical and professionally expected response.

Safe conduct of the activity

Many of the supervisory issues relevant to the safe conduct of the activity have been identified in much of what has already been said. However, when higher risk or more challenging activities take place, it is particularly important that these are appropriate for the age, needs, experiences and aptitudes of the pupils. Safety is often dependent on a progressive introduction and development of skills or experience and recommended progressions being followed. As pupils vary in their capacity to meet and respond to the activities or tasks set, allowing for differentiated inputs and outcomes is also important in the management of safety and well-being. In the outdoor environment, however, this needs to be carefully managed and controlled. Tasks that lack challenge may stimulate pupils to find their own and greater excitement – unfortunately the consequences of this are sometimes dangerous and tragic. Equally, too much challenge and perceived risk may result in negative experiences such as exhaustion, panic or fear. Particular care also needs to be taken with activities where an element of competition is generated. This could be a time limit put on a scavenger hunt or a problem-solving exercise. Time limits, penalties and other incentives can put pressure on pupils to take unnecessary risks and this needs to be considered in relation to the type of supervision, environment, etc.

Supervision issues related to the safe conduct of the activity also include the provision of appropriate facilities, equipment and clothing. The working environment and any facilities should be regularly checked and maintained to ensure that safe conditions exist. Experience has shown that in the outdoors situations can change over time and it cannot be assumed that controls designed to inform and separate people from dangers (such as fences and notices) are still present year on year. This is another reason why a pre-visit check is useful. Checks should also be made for potential hazards such as debris, protruding tree roots/stumps, overgrown ditches, forestry felling and clearance work, etc.

Any equipment used should also be checked for its condition and appropriateness in relation to regular and approved practice and the activity/location. Personal protective equipment such as hard hats, life jackets or harnesses must be fitted correctly, of the right size for the pupils and they should be instructed in its proper use. Personal clothing is also an important consideration when working out of doors. The nature of the activity, weather and time of year will influence this. For example, for some activities such as orienteering or fieldwork in woodland, long sleeves and full leg covering is advisable. The activity level of the task(s) should determine the clothing requirements and it is recommended that a water and windproof outer garment is always carried.

Any equipment used should also be appropriate for the experience of the participants and the level of the teachers'/instructors' expertise. Particular care needs to be taken if using equipment for a purpose for which it was not designed. Many problem-solving and group work activities can involve the use of non-standard equipment, e.g. milk crates, planks, fence posts, oil drums etc., and such equipment does not have clear codes of practice for its use and maintenance. Ideally such equipment should firstly be tested during a 'dry run' where safety issues and potential hazards can be anticipated.

Conclusions

This chapter has considered the management of safety in the off-site outdoor classroom and identified some of the basic principles of safe practice when working out of doors. Adequate and appropriate supervision, in its widest sense, has been shown to be fundamental not only to safe practice, but also to litigation avoidance.

It also recognises that there is more to the development of a safety culture than just increased regulation and legislation. As identified throughout this chapter, integral to safe practice is good teaching. In this respect, safe practice evolves from good practice. This said, changes in working practices are more likely to occur if teachers and others responsible for the safety of young people out of doors appreciate and understand the nature of the outdoor environment and how and why accidents happen. Learning from tragedy, the near miss experiences of others and case law can play a vital role in raising awareness of safety issues and in generating a proactive approach to safety management. However, very little attention has generally been paid to the cause of accidents and the potential benefits of learning from the experiences of others are perhaps not fully realised. In creating a safety ethos, reflection and evaluation need to become an integral part of the process. While this should occur following the activity or trip, it should also be part of a much broader and systematic approach to risk management. This should involve reviewing and revising school policies in the light of new experience and legislation.

Finally, it needs to be recognised and addressed, through policy and practice, that managing safe practice is the responsibility of several shareholders, including the pupils.

References

BAALPE (1995) *Safe Practice in Physical Education*, Dudley: Dudley LEA.

BAILIE, M. (1996) 'Risk assessments, safety statements and all that guff', *Journal of Adventure Education and Outdoor Leadership*, **13**, (3), pp. 6–7.

BERKSHIRE CC (1989) *Report of the Altwood School Inquiry Panel*, Berkshire CC.

BRACKENREG, M. (1997) 'How safe are we? A review of injury and illness in outdoor education programmes', *Journal of Adventure Education and Outdoor Leadership*, **14**, (1), pp. 10–15.

BONNINGTON, C. (1997) 'Too safe adventure under fire', *Times Educational Supplement*, October 3, p. 17.

BUCKINGHAMSHIRE CC (1985) 'School visit to Cornwall by Stoke Poges Middle School, May, 1985', *Report of Chief Education Officer*. BCC.

'Close calls – Marloes again', *Journal of Adventure Education and Outdoor Leadership*, **11**, 1, pp. 4–5.

DETR (1997) *Driver's Hours: Rules for Road Passenger Vehicles*: PSV 375, London: HMSO.

DEVON CC (1994) *Safety in Outdoor Education: Guidance and Regulations for Off-Site Activities*, Devon Learning Resources.

DEVON CC (1995) 'The Lyme Bay Canoeing Tragedy', *Report of the CEO and County Solicitor of Devon CC*. Devon CC.

DEVON LEA (1996) *A Devon Approach to Safety in Outdoor Education – Supplement Number 1*, Devon Learning Resources.

DfEE (1995) *Physical Education in the National Curriculum*, London: HMSO.

DfEE (1997) *Pupil Visits to Farms: Health Precautions*, DfEE.

DfEE (1998) *Requirements for Courses of Initial Teacher Training 4/98*, DfEE.

DfEE (1998) *Draft Guidance on Pupil Health and Safety on School Visits*, DfEE.

EVANS, J. (1994) 'Problems in the playground', *Education 3–13*, **22**, (2), pp. 34–40.

FORD, P. and BLANCHARD, J. (1993) *Leadership and Administration of Outdoor Pursuits*, PA: Venture Publishing Inc.

GREAT BRITAIN (1995) *Activity Centres (Young Persons' Safety) Act*, London: HMSO.

HALE, A. (1983) *Safety Management for Outdoor Programme Leaders.* Unpublished manuscript.

DE HAVEN, G. (1994) 'Playgrounds are all fun and games until someone loses a suit', *American City and County*, **109**, 11, p. 70.

HOUSE OF COMMONS, *Hansard.* **253**, col. 613.

HARRISON, P. and WARBURTON, P. (1993) *'Health and safety practices in schools'*, *Primary PE Focus*, Autumn, p. 3.

HEALTH AND SAFETY EXECUTIVE (1996) *A Report into Safety at Outdoor Activity Centres*, HSE Books.

JACOBS, Y. (1996) 'Safety at adventure activities centres following the Lyme Regis Tragedy: What are the Legal Consequences?' *Education and the Law*, **8**, (4), pp. 295–306.

KAISER, R. A. (1986) *Liability and Law in Recreation, Parks and Sports*, Englewood Cliffs, NJ: Prentice-Hall.

LEEDS CC (1997) *A Handbook for Educational Visits*, Leeds Education Advisory and Inspection Publishing.

LOWE, C. (1997) 'Who is responsible for what?' *Times Educational Supplement – School Management Update*, February 14, p. 15.

MOUNTAIN REPORT (1972) 'The Cairngorm Tragedy' in *Mountain, 20.*

NUT (1993) *Beyond the Classroom: Guidance on School Visits and Journeys*, London: NUT.

OFSTED (1995) *Guidance on the Inspection of Nursery and Primary Schools*, London: HMSO.

PRIEST, S. (1996) 'Thoughts on managing dangers in adventure programmes', *Journal of Adventure Education and Outdoor Leadership*, **13**, (1), pp. 18–21.

PURVES, L. (1997) 'The heights of Folly', *Times*, June 24, p. 4.

RAYMOND, C. and THOMAS, S. M. (1996) 'Safe practice: Teacher's responsibilities regarding risk', *Journal of Teacher Development*, **5**, (1), pp. 27–32.

RAYMOND, C. W. and THOMAS, S. M. (forthcoming) *Health and Safety Legislation: Teachers' Current Practice and Anxieties in Physical Education.*

RoSPA (1998) *Guide to Health and Safety at School No 5: Out and About – School Trips Part 1*, Birmingham: Royal Society for the Prevention of Accidents.

RSA, UNIVERSITY COLLEGE OF ST MARK AND ST JOHN, BAALPE (1998) *Guidelines for Delivery of Courses Leading to the Certificate in Off-Site Safety Management*, BAALPE.

Siegenthaler, K. L. (1996) 'Supervising activities for safety', *Journal of Physical Education, Recreation and Dance*, **67**, (7), pp. 29–36.

Thomas, S. M. (1994) 'Adventure education: Risk and safety out of school', in Thomas, S. M. (ed.) *Outdoor Education* Perspectives, 50: University of Exeter.

Thomas, S. M. and Raymond, C. W. (1998) 'Lessons for safety: Teachers' guide for Key Stages 1 and 2', *Child Accident Prevention Trust – Child Safety Week* 1998, CAPT.

Van de Smissen, B. (1990) *Legal Liability and Risk Management for Public and Private Entities*, **2**, Cincinnati OH: Anderson.

Watson, A. and Duff, J. (1973) 'Lessons to youth parties from the Feith Buidhe Disaster', *Climber and Rambler*, July.

Chapter 9

Organisations and resources
Carole Raymond

Throughout the text authors have frequently referred to 'regular and approved practice' (RAP) as a source of professional guidance. When charged with negligence teachers are often surprised that their competence is challenged and offer, 'I've always done it like that,' as a form of defence. However, this often reflects a lack of awareness of what should have been done in accordance with regular and approved practices (BAALPE, 1995). All subject areas have well-established teaching practices and procedures that over the years have avoided foreseeable accidents without reducing the challenge and developmental value of the activities for pupils.

As subjects change and new ways of working evolve, e.g. promoting greater independence for pupils and making use of ICT, so teachers need to try and keep up-to-date with what is currently regular and approved practice. Opportunities for in-service and on-going professional developments are variable, and so teachers have to accept some responsibility to ensure they keep up to date. Various opportunities include:
- Working with student teachers
- Creating networks in local education authorities and sharing good practice ideas
- Making sure colleagues who attend courses disseminate information when they return to school (newsletter/notice-board/seminar)
- Keeping a data base of organisations and resources.

Finding time for keeping abreast of health and safety and regular and improved practice must be a priority for all teachers.

Organisations - Useful contacts (for resources and information)

Association for Science Education, Lecturers College Lane, Hatfield, Herts AL10 9AA; tel: 01701 267411

Child Accident Prevention Trust, 4th Floor Clerks Court 18–20 Farringdon Lane, London EC12 3AU; tel: 0171 608 3828

Consortium of Local Education Authorities for the Provision of School Science (CLEAPS), Brunel University, Uxbridge UB8 3PH; tel: 01895 251496

Hazard Alley, The Safety Centre (MK)Ltd, 18 Careters Lane, Kiln Farm, Milton Keynes MK11 3ES; tel: 01908 263009

British Association of Advisers in Physical Education (BAALPE), Nelson House, 6 The Beacon, Exmouth, Devon EX8 2AG; tel: 01395 263247

DfEE Publications Centre, PO Box 5050, Sudbury, Suffolk CO10 6ZQ; tel: 0845 6022260; fax: 0845 6033360

Health Education Authority (HEA), Health Promotion Information Centre, Hamilton House, Mabledon Place, London WC1H 9TX; tel: 0171 383 3833

Health and Safety Executive Information Centres

London, Rose Court 2 Southwark Bridge, London SE1 9HS;

Sheffield, PO Box 1999, Broad Lane, Sheffield S3 7HQ; Infoline tel: 0541 545500 fax: 0114 289 2333

home web page: http://www.open.gov.uk/hse/hsehome.htm

HSE Books PO Box 1999, Customer Services Dept, Sudbury, Suffolk CO10 6FS; tel: 01787 881165; fax: 01787 313995

HMSO Publications, PO Box 276, London SW8 5DT; tel: (orders) 0171 873 9090; (enquiries) 0171 873 0011

HSE Bootle Information Centre, St Hugh's House, Stanley Precinct, Bootle, Merseyside L20 3QY

Institute of Home Safety, Christine Eaton, Sec, 73 Westhill Drive, Dartford, Kent DA1 6FA; tel: 0181 312 5875

Kidscape, 152 Buckingham Palace
Road, London SW1W 9TR;
tel: 0171 730 3300

National Play Information Centre
(NPIC), 199 Knightsbridge, London
SW7 1DE; tel: 0171 584 6464

National Playing Fields Association
(NPFA), 25 Ovington Square,
London SW3 1LQ;
tel: 0171 584 6445

Scottish Schools Equipment
Research Centre (SSERC), 24 Bernard
Terrace, Edinburgh EH8 9NX

Royal Society for the Prevention of
Accidents (ROSPA), Egbaston Park,
353 Bristol Road, Birmingham B5
7ST; tel: 0171-972 2000

Reading and resources

Child Accident Prevention Trust

Accident Prevention Resource Guide (1996) London: CAPT – Section 1
suggests how to conduct research into safety issues. Section 2 identifies
selected organisations, the work they undertake and the resources produced.
Section 3 offers a sample of resources on different issues.

The Risk Pack – focuses on accident prevention and risk. Teachers notes and
suggestions for pupil activities across the curriculum for KS2.

Croner Publications (1996) *Teacher's Briefing The Teacher's Legal Guide*

'Schools Health and Safety Management – Records and Procedures'

'Guidelines for Schools and Teachers on Health and Safety in Schools'

'Bulletin (1993 No.3) Health and Safety: The New Regulations'

Department for Education and Employment

School Governors – A Guide to the Law

Guidance on First Aid for Schools: A good practice guide (1998)

*Administering Medicine – Supporting Pupils with Medical Needs – A good
practice guide*

Circular 14/96 *Supporting Pupils with Medical Needs in School*

Activity Centres – Circular 22/94 *Safety in Outdoor Activity Centres: Guidance*

Child Protection – Circular 9/93 *Protection of Children: Disclosure of Criminal Background of those with Access to Children*; Circular 10/95 *Protecting children from Abuse: the role of the Education Service*; Circular 11/95 *Misconduct of Teachers and Workers with Children and Young Persons*

Draft Guidance on Pupil Health and Safety on School Visits (1998)

School Discipline – Circular 8/94 *The Education of Children with Emotional and Behavioural Difficulties* – Circular 10/94 *Exclusions from School*

School Security – DfEE (1997) *Dealing with Troublemakers Protecting Pupils and Staff Using the Law*

Sickness – Circular 13/93 *Phyiscal and Mental Fitness to Teach of Teachers and of Entrants to Initial Teacher Training*

Teachers' Qualifications – Circular 18/89 *The Education (Teachers) Regulations 1989*

Teaching: High Status, High Standards. Requirements for Courses of Initial Teacher Training – Circular 4/98 1998

Teachers Pay and Conditions – Circular 4/96 *School Teachers Pay and Conditions of Employment 1996*

Health and Safety Commission (HSC)/Executive (HSE)

Steps to Successful Health and Safety Management: Special help for directors and managers IND(G)132L – free leaflet

Five Steps to Risk Assessment: A step-by-step guide to a safer and healthier workplace 1994 IND(G) – free leaflet or available in priced packs £5 for 10, ISBN 07 176 0904 0

A Guide to Risk Assessment Requirements: Common provision in health and safety law (1996) IND(G)18 – free leaflet or available in priced packs, ISBN 07176 12 112

Everyone's Guide to RIDDOR '95 (1996) HSE31 – free leaflet or available in priced packs, ISBN 07 17610772

Reporting School Accidents (1997) EDIS 1 – free information sheet

Workplace Health, Safety and Welfare Regulations 1992 (1995) IACL97 – free leaflet or available in priced packs, ISBN 0 7176 1049 7

Workplace Health, Safety and Welfare – A short guide (1995) – free leaflet or available in priced packs, ISBN 0 7176 0890 *5 Essentials of health and safety at work* (1994), ISBN 0 7176 0716X, £5.95

Signposts to Safety Signs Regulations (1996) IND(G) 184 – free leaflet or available in priced packs, ISBN 0 7176 1139 6

List of Current Health and Safety Legislation 1996 – Book and disk, ISBN 0 7176 13119 £11.95

Health education authority

Health for Life 1 – A teacher's guide, topic suggestions and work sheets, for children 4–11 years, £28.25

Health for Life 2 – A teacher's guide on three topics: drugs, keeping safe and relationships. The activities suggested conform to national curriculum requirements

RoSPA

Child Safety Starter Pack – Materials for teaching home safety. Includes information sheets, statistics and a selection of leaflets, £12.50

Streets Ahead – Teaching ideas for integrated safety education programmes. Includes cross curricular worksheets and activities on road safety, £48

Guide to Health and Safety at School No 5: Out and About – School Trips, Part 1

Appendix	# Physical education health and safety audit – checklist

School -- Date of Audit --

A – Organisation and management

YES   NO

		YES	NO
A1	There is a Health and Safety policy with reference to the Code of Practice Document	☐	☐
A2	There is a clear written scheme for delegating functions and responsibilities	☐	☐
A3	These delegated responsibilities are understood and accepted by staff and volunteers	☐	☐
A4	There are clear established channels of communications for new safety requirements to be brought to the attention of staff and volunteers	☐	☐
A5	There are clear established channels of communication for safety problems encountered by staff to be referred back to managers, e.g. faulty equipment, etc	☐	☐
A6	Clear notices are displayed in all appropriate areas to inform users of H&S issues relating to specific facility usage	☐	☐
A7	All staff receive formal training in PE-specific safety issues	☐	☐
A8	Staff training in safety issues is monitored	☐	☐
A9	Routine training and updating in H&S issues occurs through departmental meetings and staff development days	☐	☐
A10	There is a budget for H&S material and staff training	☐	☐
A11	There is regular monitoring of safety procedures for indoor and outdoor activities	☐	☐
A12	Teaching group sizes are appropriate for the activities	☐	☐
A13	(a) staff:pupil ratios are appropriate for: swimming	☐	☐
	ski trips	☐	☐
	residentials	☐	☐
	(b) the school is aware of appropriate staff:pupil ratios for activities covered	☐	☐

A14 *Staff contributing to PE*

    (a) number of staff with specialist training

    (b) number of staff with coaching qualifications

    (c) number of non-specialist staff with in-service training

    (d) number of non-specialists with no qualifications

    (e) Supply staff are used for residential visits | YES | NO |

    (f) NQTs receive induction on a regular basis | YES | NO |

    (g) Number of AOTTs contributing to: curriculum

                              extra-curriculum

    (h) AOTTs receive clear written guidance re responsibilities | YES | NO |

    (i) the school has a policy for AOTTs | YES | NO |

    (j) Police check is conducted on all AOTTs | YES | NO |

A15 *Pupil supervision and control*

    (a) pupils are supervised for changing | always | sometimes | never |

    (b) control within lesson is | satisfactory | unsatisfactory |

    (c) pupils are taught to carry equipment | YES | NO |

    (d) pupils lift and carry equipment | correctly | incorrectly |

A16 *Facilities*   YES   NO

    (a) off-site facilities are used for: curriculum activities

                              extra-curricular activities

    (b) residential centres are used for: curriculum activities

                              extra-curricular activities

    (c) governor permission is sought

    (d) full checks are made pre-visit

A17 *Equipment*

    (a) hazardous substances are stored correctly

    (b) dangerous equipment (e.g. javelins, trampoline, archery) is stored separately

    Primary Schools only

    (c) equipment is appropriate for the age of the children

    (d) equipment is appropriately stored in the hall

    (e) equipment is safely stored in the hall

A18 *Firearms*

    (a) starting pistols – the department has firing pistol(s)

    (b) they are stored in a suitably locked cupboard

    (c) ammunition is stored separately

    (d) staff using starting pistols have received training

A19 *Risk Assessment*

    (a) there is a specific risk assessment policy in the school or department

    (b) risk assessment is included in: schemes of work

                            lesson plans

    (c) risk assessment covers all areas of the curriculum including:

	satisfactory	unsatisfactory
use of multi gyms		
off-site activities, e.g. orienteering		

    (d) risk assessment for sample activities (e.g. summer – athletics; winter: trampoline, rugby) is: satisfactory | unsatisfactory

B – *Documentation, records and monitoring*

B1 (a) emergency and accident procedures are documented   YES | NO

    (b) accidents are reported and recorded   YES | NO

    (c) who deals with accidents: within lessons

                         during other activities

(d) there is a member of the PE staff with a current First Aid certificate   YES | NO

    Name(s) of staff with First Aid Certificates

B2 Essential documentation is available to all staff: YES   NO

    (a) Departmental policy

    (b) Safe Practice in PE – BAALPE

    (c) LEA Guidelines for Safety in PE

B3 There is a system for notifying teachers of pupils' medical conditions

B4 Staff are aware of the procedures and medication requirements for pupils in their care

B5 There are departmental records of safety checks: internal

                                          external

B6 (a) name of the company used to check gymnastics equipment

    (b) frequency of this inspection

    (c) date of last inspection

(d) name(s) of teacher(s) responsible for checking the safety equipment (e.g. cricket, hockey safety items)

$$\boxed{}$$

(e) what is the frequency of safety checks on all equipment (e.g. javelins, hurdles, trampoline)

$$\boxed{}$$

C – General

C1 designated FIRE EXITS are clearly marked

C2 Fire exit procedures are displayed in every indoor PE area

C3 Fire exit routes are kept free from obstruction

C4 a First Aid kit and blanket are available in each indoor working area

C5 a First Aid kit and blanket are available during extra-curricular activities

C6 pupils are appropriately clothed for physical activities

C7 jewellery is removed for physical activity

C8 protective/safety equipment is provided where necessary (e.g. cricket, hockey guards)

C9 facilities are regularly cleaned to a satisfactory standard

C10 outside playing surfaces are in good, safe condition

C11 changing rooms are: clean

                   well maintained

C12 showering facilities are in good, safe condition

C13 Select 2 or 3 activities

Activity	1	2	3
(a) content is suitable for age, ability/experience	Y:N	Y:N	Y:N
(b) delivery is suitable for age, ability/experience	Y:N	Y:N	Y:N
(c) equipment is suitable for age, ability/experience	Y:N	Y:N	Y:N
(d) staff:pupil ratio is appropriate for the activity	Y:N	Y:N	Y:N

Ref: Northamptonshire Education and Community Learning (1998)

Notes on contributors

Carole Raymond is a Director of the National Unit of Safety across the Curriculum (NUSAC) and Lecturer in physical education at the University of Exeter. She has been involved in initial teacher training of teachers and in the professional development of experienced teachers for many years. Her specialist areas include pedagogy, curriculum development and management. More recently she has trained as an expert witness and is a representative on the BAALPE Expert Witness Institute. She is the editor of the BAALPE national journal and author of *Coordinating Physical Education across the Primary School* (Falmer 1998).

Peter Whitlam is senior secondary inspector for Dudley LEA with additional responsibility for physical education. Peter has worked in schools, higher education and for the advisory inspectorate and has provided inservice courses across the country as well as overseas. He has a law degree and has much experience as an expert witness. He is also deputy safety officer for BAALPE.

John Twyford has responsibility for design and technology at the University of Exeter. He has experience of both primary and secondary education and is actively involved in teachers continuing professional development. He has published in various journals and is author of *Design, Capability and Awareness* (Longman 1994).

Chris Taylor is a lecturer in education at the University of Exeter. His specialist area is ICT, with a particular interest in primary education. He previously was a primary class teacher and worked in the Computer Advisory Service for Kent County Council. A particular concern is the potential health risk of VDU equipment, and he has undertaken research looking at electromagnetic emissions from computers commonly used in education.

Nigel Skinner is a lecturer in science education at the University of Exeter where he is involved in training both primary and secondary science specialists. Safety is a particular interest of his and he has been a member of the Exeter University Safety Committee for 7 years. He has been a junior school governor for 8 years and is currently the Chair of the Association for Science Education (South West Region).

Sue Thomas is Assistant Director of Initial Professional Studies at the School of Education, University of Exeter. She also lectures in physical education and outdoor education to Initial Teacher Education students. Prior to this she taught both areas in schools where she gained extensive experience of working with pupils and teachers in the outdoor classroom. Sue is also a Director of the National Unit for Safety across the Curriculum (NUSAC), a tutor for the Certificate in Off-Site Safety Management Course and a member of the BAALPE Expert Witness Institute. Her research interests have included health and safety in physical education focusing on teachers' practice and concerns.

Index